HOUSING ISSUES, LAWS AND PROGRAMS

VETERAN HOUSING ASSISTANCE

LOANS, GRANTS, AND HOMELESSNESS PROGRAMS

HOUSING ISSUES, LAWS AND PROGRAMS

Additional books in this series can be found on Nova's website under the Series tab.

Additional E-books in this series can be found on Nova's website under the E-book tab.

MILITARY AND VETERAN ISSUES

Additional books in this series can be found on Nova's website under the Series tab.

Additional E-books in this series can be found on Nova's website under the E-book tab.

HOUSING ISSUES, LAWS AND PROGRAMS

VETERAN HOUSING ASSISTANCE

LOANS, GRANTS, AND HOMELESSNESS PROGRAMS

CRAIG DEL MONTE
EDITOR

nova
publishers
New York

Copyright © 2013 by Nova Science Publishers, Inc.

For permission to use material from this book please contact us:
Telephone 631-231-7269; Fax 631-231-8175
Web Site: http://www.novapublishers.com

NOTICE TO THE READER

The Publisher has taken reasonable care in the preparation of this book, but makes no expressed or implied warranty of any kind and assumes no responsibility for any errors or omissions. No liability is assumed for incidental or consequential damages in connection with or arising out of information contained in this book. The Publisher shall not be liable for any special, consequential, or exemplary damages resulting, in whole or in part, from the readers' use of, or reliance upon, this material. Any parts of this book based on government reports are so indicated and copyright is claimed for those parts to the extent applicable to compilations of such works.

Independent verification should be sought for any data, advice or recommendations contained in this book. In addition, no responsibility is assumed by the publisher for any injury and/or damage to persons or property arising from any methods, products, instructions, ideas or otherwise contained in this publication.

This publication is designed to provide accurate and authoritative information with regard to the subject matter covered herein. It is sold with the clear understanding that the Publisher is not engaged in rendering legal or any other professional services. If legal or any other expert assistance is required, the services of a competent person should be sought. FROM A DECLARATION OF PARTICIPANTS JOINTLY ADOPTED BY A COMMITTEE OF THE AMERICAN BAR ASSOCIATION AND A COMMITTEE OF PUBLISHERS.

Additional color graphics may be available in the e-book version of this book.

Library of Congress Cataloging-in-Publication Data

ISBN: 978-1-62417-369-1

Published by Nova Science Publishers, Inc. ✝ *New York*

CONTENTS

PREFACE

The Department of Veterans Affairs (VA) has assisted veterans with homeownership since 1944, when Congress enacted the loan guaranty program to help veterans returning from World War II purchase homes. The loan guaranty program assists veterans by insuring mortgages made by private lenders, and is available for the purchase or construction of homes as well as to refinance existing loans. A third way in which the VA provides housing assistance to both veterans and active duty service members is through the Specially Adapted Housing (SAH) Program. Through the SAH program, veterans with certain service-connected disabilities may obtain grants from the VA to purchase or remodel homes to fit their needs. This book discusses these three types of housing assistance; the loan guaranty program, direct loan programs, and Specially Adapted Housing program--their origins, how they operate, and how they are funded. Additionally, the default and foreclosure of VA-guaranteed loans is discussed.

Chapter 1 – The loan guaranty has expanded over the years so that it is available to (1) all veterans who fulfill specific duration of service requirements or who were released from active duty due to service-connected disabilities, (2) members of the reserves who completed at least six years of service, and (3) spouses of veterans who died in action or of service-connected disabilities. Under the loan guaranty, the VA agrees to reimburse lenders for a portion of losses if borrowers default. Unlike insurance provided through the Federal Housing Administration (FHA) insurance program, the VA does not insure 100% of the loan, and instead the percentage of the loan that is guaranteed is based on the principal balance of the loan.

Veterans who enter into VA-guaranteed loans must pay an up-front fee based on a number of factors that include the type of loan entered into (for example purchase or refinance), whether service was active duty or in the reserves, whether the loan is the first or subsequent VA loan a borrower has entered into, and the amount of down payment. Borrowers are not required to make a down payment for a VA-guaranteed loan, but the up-front fee is reduced if there is a down payment of 5% or more. Most borrowers (88% in FY2011) do not make a down payment.

Chapter 2 – The wars in Iraq and Afghanistan have brought renewed attention to the needs of veterans, including the needs of homeless veterans. Both male and female veterans have been overrepresented in the homeless population, and as the number of veterans increases due to these conflicts, there is concern that the number of homeless veterans could rise commensurately. The recent economic downturn also has raised concerns that homelessness could increase among all groups, including veterans.

Congress has created numerous programs that serve homeless veterans specifically, almost all of which are funded through the Veterans Health Administration. These programs provide health care and rehabilitation services for homeless veterans (the Health Care for Homeless Veterans and Domiciliary Care for Homeless Veterans programs), employment assistance (Homeless Veterans Reintegration Program and Compensated Work Therapy program), and transitional housing (Grant and Per Diem program) as well as other supportive services. The VA also works with the Department of Housing and Urban Development (HUD) to provide permanent supportive housing to homeless veterans through the HUD-VA Supported Housing Program (HUD-VASH). In the HUD-VASH program, HUD funds rental assistance through Section 8 vouchers while the VA provides supportive services. In addition, two newly enacted programs focus on homelessness prevention through supportive services: the VA's Supportive Services for Veteran Families program and a VA and HUD homelessness prevention demonstration program.

Chapter 3 – According to a HUD and VA report, veterans are overrepresented among the homeless population. The HUD-VASH program combines rental assistance for homeless veterans in the form of section 8 Housing Choice vouchers provided by HUD with case management and clinical services provided by VA at VAMCs and community-based outpatient clinics. This collaborative initiative between the two agencies is intended to target the most vulnerable, most needy, and chronically homeless veterans. GAO was asked to examine (1) how VA and HUD determine veteran eligibility for HUD-VASH, (2) what data VA and HUD collect and report on HUD-VASH and their data reliability efforts, and (3) what is known about HUD-VASH performance.

To address these objectives, GAO reviewed HUD-VASH program requirements and reported program data through March 2012; and interviewed VA and HUD headquarters officials, staff at a non-representative sample of 10 VAMCs and 10 PHAs, and representatives of organizations that advocate for veterans or individuals experiencing homelessness.

GAO makes no recommendations in this report. HUD, VA, and the U.S. Interagency Council on Homelessness generally agreed with GAO's conclusions.

Chapter 4 – A broad range of benefits are offered to veterans of the U.S. Armed Forces and to certain members of their families by the U.S. Department of Veterans Affairs (VA). Among these benefits are various types of financial assistance, including monthly cash payments to disabled veterans, health care, education, and housing benefits. Basic criteria must be met to be eligible to receive any of the benefits administered by the VA.

For a former servicemember to receive certain VA benefits, the person must have active U.S. military service for a minimum period of time and meet nature of discharge requirements. Some members of the National Guard and reserve components have difficulty meeting the active duty and length of service requirements. However, a member of the National Guard or reserve components who is activated for federal military service and serves the full period of activation is considered a veteran for purposes of VA benefits.

In: Veteran Housing Assistance   ISBN: 978-1-62417-369-1
Editor: Craig Del Monte   © 2013 Nova Science Publishers, Inc.

Chapter 1

VA HOUSING: GUARANTEED LOANS, DIRECT LOANS, AND SPECIALLY ADAPTED HOUSING GRANTS*

Libby Perl

SUMMARY

The loan guaranty has expanded over the years so that it is available to (1) all veterans who fulfill specific duration of service requirements or who were released from active duty due to service-connected disabilities, (2) members of the reserves who completed at least six years of service, and (3) spouses of veterans who died in action or of service-connected disabilities. Under the loan guaranty, the VA agrees to reimburse lenders for a portion of losses if borrowers default. Unlike insurance provided through the Federal Housing Administration (FHA) insurance program, the VA does not insure 100% of the loan, and instead the percentage of the loan that is guaranteed is based on the principal balance of the loan (see **Table 3**).

Veterans who enter into VA-guaranteed loans must pay an up-front fee based on a number of factors that include the type of loan entered into (for example purchase or refinance), whether service was active duty or in the reserves, whether the loan is the first or subsequent VA loan a borrower has

---

* This is an edited, reformatted and augmented version of the Congressional Research Service Publication, CRS Report for Congress R42504, dated April 24, 2012.

entered into, and the amount of down payment (see **Table 6**). Borrowers are not required to make a down payment for a VA-guaranteed loan, but the up-front fee is reduced if there is a down payment of 5% or more. Most borrowers (88% in FY2011) do not make a down payment.

In addition to guaranteeing loans from private lenders, the VA also makes direct loans to borrowers in certain circumstances. The original VA direct loan, which was targeted to veterans in rural areas, is now available only to veterans or servicemembers with certain service-connected disabilities. Another direct loan program, originally enacted as a demonstration program in 1992, serves Native American veterans, including veterans living in American Samoa, Guam, and the Commonwealth of the Northern Mariana Islands. In addition, the VA may enter into direct loans in cases where a borrower is delinquent or defaults on a VA-guaranteed loan. The VA may either acquire a loan from a lender and continue servicing itself (called "acquired loans") or, in cases of foreclosure, the VA may purchase the property and resell it. In these cases, the VA may enter into a loan with a purchaser whether he or she is a veteran or not (called "vendee loans").

A third way in which the VA provides housing assistance to both veterans and active duty servicemembers is through the Specially Adapted Housing (SAH) Program. Through the SAH program, veterans with certain service-connected disabilities may obtain grants from the VA to purchase or remodel homes to fit their needs. The amount of a grant depends on the disability, and in some cases grants can be used to modify the homes of family members with whom veterans or servicemembers are staying (see **Table 7**).

This chapter discusses these three types of housing assistance—the loan guaranty program, direct loan programs, and Specially Adapted Housing program—their origins, how they operate, and how they are funded. The chapter also has a section that discusses the default and foreclosure of VA-guaranteed loans.

INTRODUCTION

The U.S. Department of Veterans Affairs (VA) administers several programs that assist individual veterans in purchasing and/or rehabilitating homes. The specific ways in which the VA assists veterans include (1) guaranteeing home mortgages from private lenders (through the Loan Guaranty Program, a form of insurance) to help veterans obtain financing for home purchases, improvements, or refinancing; (2) providing direct loans for home purchases to Native American veterans and to purchasers of homes that are in the VA inventory due to default and foreclosure; and (3) extending grants and loans to veterans with service-connected disabilities so that they can adapt housing to fit their needs through the Specially Adapted Housing Program.

This report discusses some of the legislative history behind each of these housing programs, and provides details about how the programs currently operate. There is a separate section on funding for VA loan programs, and the final section of the report discusses VA efforts to assist borrowers who face default and foreclosure. While the VA also provides housing assistance for homeless veterans, this report does not address these programs. For more information about homeless veterans and programs that assist them, see *Veterans and Homelessness*, by Libby Perl.

THE VA LOAN GUARANTY PROGRAM

The VA Loan Guaranty Program is a mortgage insurance program through which eligible veterans enter into mortgages with private lenders, and the VA guarantees that it will pay lenders a portion of losses that may be suffered as a result of borrower default. VA-guaranteed loans are available for the purchase, construction, or repair/rehabilitation of a "dwelling"—defined to include homes with up to four units, single condominium units, and manufactured homes classified as real property[1]—or a farm and farm residence. The guaranty is also available to finance the purchase of a manufactured home not classified as real property, and to refinance an existing loan.

The VA loan guaranty came about as an alternative to a cash bonus for veterans returning from World War II, considered less expensive than a bonus, but still a way to provide benefits to veterans.[2] Credit was seen as one of the areas where veterans were at a disadvantage compared to their non-veteran counterparts because they had not had the time to establish a career or credit history that would allow them to obtain a mortgage without a guaranty.[3] The Servicemen's Readjustment Act of 1944 (P.L. 78-346) created the loan guaranty as part of a package of benefits for returning veterans. The act also included educational benefits (the 1944 Act introduced the GI Bill), employment counseling and placement services, and payments for unemployed veterans. The package of benefits was meant to help veterans reintegrate into the civilian economy.[4] The law provided that the VA would guaranty loans for veterans to purchase or construct a home, purchase a farm or farm equipment, or purchase a business. The guaranty was limited to the greater of 50% of the loan or $2,000, and loans could not have an interest rate above 4%. The VA paid the interest on the guaranteed portion of the loan during its first year. Veterans had the greater of two years from the termination of the war, or two years from their date of separation from the military, to apply.

Within a year, Congress amended the loan guaranty to address some of the aspects of the program that did not seem to be working (P.L. 79-268). The maximum guaranty was raised to $4,000 (prices of homes had risen), the maximum maturity was increased from 20 to 25 years (the shorter maturity period had resulted in higher payments), and veterans were given 10 years from the end of the war to apply (2 years had been too short a time frame).[5]

Over time, the loan guaranty has been expanded to include all veterans who served on active duty from World War II on, with varying length of service requirements, as well as those who served in the selected reserves; the amount of the guaranty has grown; business purchases are no longer eligible and farm purchases have been limited; and the uses have expanded to include refinancing, energy efficiency improvements, and the purchase of manufactured homes. This section of the report describes eligibility for the loan guaranty ("Borrower Eligibility"), ways in which it can be used ("Uses of the Loan Guaranty"), coverage ("Amount of Coverage Provided by the Loan Guaranty"), and how the VA loan guaranty differs from the Federal Housing Administration (FHA) mortgage insurance program ("How the VA Loan Guaranty Differs from FHA Insurance").

Borrower Eligibility

Service Criteria

Veteran eligibility for the VA loan guaranty started narrowly, targeted to individuals who served during World War II. As additional conflicts arose, veterans of those conflicts, as well as peacetime eras, were made eligible for the program.

A veteran is defined as "a person who served in the active military, naval, or air service, and who was discharged or released therefrom under conditions other than dishonorable."[6] To be eligible for VA loan benefits (and most other VA benefits), veterans must fulfill specific time period and duration of service requirements. In addition, reservists with at least six years of service are eligible for the loan guaranty.[7] Reservists need not have served on active duty, unlike what is required for some other veterans benefits, as long as they fulfill the duration of service requirement. In addition, the spouses of veterans who died in action, died of a service-connected disability, or who are missing in action, captured, or forcibly detained are eligible for the loan guaranty. See Table 1 for a complete list of eligibility categories.[8]

Financial Criteria

In addition to length of service requirements, the VA loan guaranty has underwriting criteria designed to ensure that veterans have the financial means to make mortgage payments. The statute gives the VA Secretary the authority to set underwriting standards in regulation, which are further supplemented by the *VA Lenders Handbook*.[9] The underwriting standards consider a veteran's income, expenses, and credit history in determining whether he or she qualifies for a guaranteed loan. In seeking to balance income and expenses, a veteran must meet requirements established via a debt-to-income ratio standard and a residual income analysis.

- **Debt-to-Income Ratio:** In the debt-to-income analysis, a lender is to look at the ratio of a veteran's anticipated housing expenses and other long-term monthly obligations compared to his or her stable and reliable monthly income.[10] To be stable and reliable, income is to be expected to continue "for the foreseeable future." Examples of unreliable income include VA education benefits, unemployment compensation, and irregular overtime pay.[11] A veteran's total debt-to-income ratio should not exceed 41%, although there are provisions to allow for exceptions to this requirement in cases where a lender is able to justify the loan to the VA.
- **Residual Income:** The residual income test is used to determine whether a veteran's income after payments for shelter expenses and other debts is adequate to meet living expenses. Unlike the debt-to-income ratio, the residual income test looks at additional expenses such as food, clothing, health care, and gasoline that are not captured as part of debt.[12] The loan guaranty regulations contain a guide to sufficient residual income by region.[13]

The Loan Guaranty Program does not require veterans to have a specific credit score to qualify for a loan, but the underwriting guidelines require lenders to analyze a borrower's credit history.[14] Lenders must be able to explain decisions to extend credit to borrowers who have an adverse credit history, and certain situations, such as an unpaid court-ordered judgment or a bankruptcy within the previous one or two years, may disqualify a borrower from obtaining a guaranteed loan. A previous foreclosure is not a bar to obtaining a VA-guaranteed loan, but borrowers who had previous VA-guaranteed loans that were foreclosed upon may have to repay the government for any losses suffered prior to obtaining a new loan.[15]

Table 1. Service Eligibility for the Loan Guaranty

Eligibility Category	Public Law Initiating Eligibility[a]	Time Requirement (if any)
Active Duty[b] Service during World War II (9/16/40 to 7/25/47)	P.L. 78-346	90 days[c]
Active Duty Service during the Korean Conflict (6/27/50 to 1/31/55)	P.L. 82-550	90 days[c]
Active Duty Service during the Vietnam Era (8/5/64 to 5/7/75)	P.L. 95-476	90 days[c]
Active Duty Service Post- • World War II (7/26/47 to 6/26/50) • Korea (2/1/55 to 8/4/64) • Vietnam (5/8/75 to 8/1/90[d])	P.L. 100-322	181 days
Service Begun After[e] • 9/7/80 (enlisted personnel) or • 10/16/81 (officers[f])	P.L. 97-66	• 24 months or • full period ordered to active duty, but no less than 181 days during peacetime or 90 days[c] during wartime
Service in the Selected Reserve[g]	P.L. 102-547	720 days (six years)
Released from Active Duty or Selected Reserve due to Service-Connected Disability (any service after 9/15/40)	P.L. 78-346	—
Spouse of a Veteran who Died in Action or of a Service-Connected Disability Who Has Not Remarried[h]	P.L. 81-475	—
Spouse of Member of Active Duty Military who • is missing in action, • captured, or • forcibly detained	P.L. 91-584	—

Source: 38 U.S.C. §§3701-3702, 38 U.S.C. §5303A, and U.S. Department of Veterans Affairs, *Manual M26-1 Guaranteed Loan Processing Manual*, September 16, 1996, pp. 2-1 to 2-28, http://www.benefits.va.gov/warms/ M26_1.asp.

Note: The two categories not included in the table are (1) sole surviving child in a family where a parent or sibling was killed while in the Armed Forces, captured or missing in action, or permanently disabled and (2) in some circumstances, commissioned officers of the Public Health Service and the National Oceanic and Atmospheric Administration.

a. Subsequent laws may have extended the period of service or otherwise modified eligibility requirements.

b. Active duty service refers to full time service in the Army, Navy, Air Force, Marines, or Coast Guard.

c. A veteran qualifies if any part of his or her 90 days of service was during wartime.

d. While the Vietnam era extends to August 1, 1990, benefits for veterans who began service after September 7, 1980, are subject to 38 U.S.C. §5303A(b). See tablenote e.

e. 38 U.S.C. §5303A(b). The two-year minimum service requirement for many veterans' benefits was added to the law in 1980 as part of P.L. 96-342, the Department of Defense Authorization Act of 1981.

A year later, P.L. 97-66, the Veterans' Disability Compensation, Housing, and Memorial Benefits Amendments of 1981, amended the law to include officers as well as enlisted personnel, and to exempt those discharged for reduction-in-force purposes.

Congress was concerned that "excessive numbers of servicemembers were, through inappropriate or unproductive conduct, bringing about their early discharges, that many of them had enlisted for the purpose of obtaining eligibility for veterans' benefits based on short periods of service, and that it is wasteful for the Federal government to provide veterans' benefits to those who fail substantially to fulfill their active-duty service commitments." U.S. Congress, Senate Committee on Veterans' Affairs, *Veterans' Disability Compensation, Housing, and Memorial Benefits Amendments of 1981*, report to accompany S. 917, 97th Cong., 1st sess., July 16, 1981, S.Rept. 97-153, pp. 36-37.

f. The dates for officers and enlisted personnel differ because the original law implementing the 24-month length-of-service requirement (P.L. 96-342) only applied to enlisted personnel and not officers. See U.S. Congress, House Committee on Veterans' Affairs, *Veterans' Compensation Amendments of 1981*, report to accompany H.R. 3995, 97th Cong., 1st sess., July 16, 1981, H.Rept. 97-179, pp. 20-21. P.L. 97-66 amended the law to apply to officers.

g. The Selected Reserve includes the Army, Navy, Air Force, Marine Corps, and Coast Guard Reserves, the Army National Guard, and the Air National Guard. 10 U.S.C. §10101.

h. The term "surviving spouse" is defined at 38 U.S.C. §101 to mean someone who has not remarried.

Uses of the Loan Guaranty

Financing the Purchase, Construction, or Improvement of Dwellings or Farm Residences

Loan guarantees are available for the purchase or construction, or to make improvements (including energy efficiency improvements) to either a "dwelling" or farm residence.[16] A dwelling is defined as a building primarily used and occupied as a home (defined as a "place of residence")[17], and that consists of no more than four single family units (under most circumstances)[18], one of which will be occupied by an eligible veteran. While a daily physical presence is not necessary to occupy the property as a home, occupancy of the property must be more than intermittent.[19] For example, the property should be near a borrower's place of employment, and if his or her job requires an absence for a "substantial amount of time," there must be a history of continuous presence in the community prior to the absence, and there should be no attempt to establish a principal residence elsewhere.[20] Use of a property as a vacation home would not qualify for the VA loan guaranty.

A range of housing qualifies as a dwelling for VA loan guaranty purposes. A single condominium unit qualifies as a dwelling, and a manufactured home may also be a dwelling if the veteran owns the land to which it is affixed and the state classifies it as real property.[21] Note, however, that a manufactured home that does not meet these requirements may qualify separately under the manufactured housing section of the law (for more information, see the next section of this report entitled "Loan Guaranty for Manufactured Housing"). The loan guaranty can also include the purchase of land for both the construction of a single-family home[22] or for placement of a manufactured home.[23]

In addition to purchasing property, an eligible veteran may enter into a guaranteed loan for the construction of housing or to make improvements to property the veteran already owns. In general, the loan guaranty cannot be used to purchase a property that requires significant work (i.e., a fixer-upper) due to minimum property standards for homes purchased with VA-guaranteed loans.[24] However, if a property meets minimum property standards, and a veteran wants to include funds for improvements in a purchase money loan, the appraiser is to take the value of the improvements into account, increasing the loan amount for which a borrower could potentially qualify.[25] The loan guaranty can also be used for loans to make "energy efficiency improvements" to a property a veteran is purchasing or to a property already owned. Energy efficiency improvements were added as a permissible use of the loan guaranty in 1978 as part of the Veterans' Housing Benefits Act (P.L. 95-476). Energy efficiency improvements are limited to $6,000, and may include such things as solar heating and cooling or conservation measures, such as insulation, weatherizing, and furnace replacement.[26]

Loan Guaranty for Manufactured Housing

The VA loan guaranty has evolved so that there are two ways in which manufactured housing is classified and guaranteed. First, as mentioned in the previous section, manufactured housing can be classified as a dwelling that may be guaranteed under the regular guaranty provisions of the statute (38 U.S.C. §3710). In addition, it can be classified and guaranteed under a separate manufactured housing portion of the law (38 U.S.C. §3712). Congress created the latter program first in 1970 (see the Veterans' Housing Act of 1970, P.L. 91-506), and later specified that manufactured housing could be included as a dwelling for the regular guaranty provisions in Section 3710 (see the Veterans' Compensation and Program Improvements Amendments of 1984, P.L. 98-223). Despite this flexibility, it appears that the VA has not guaranteed new manufactured housing loans under Section 3712 of the law since 1996.[27]

The VA has slightly different definitions for manufactured housing based on the portion of the statute under which it is guaranteed. The definitions share in common that manufactured housing is

> [a] movable dwelling unit designed and constructed for year-round occupancy on land by a single family, which dwelling unit contains permanent eating, cooking, sleeping, and sanitary facilities. A double-wide manufactured home is a movable dwelling designed for occupancy by one family consisting of (1) two or more units intended to be joined together horizontally when located on a site, but capable of independent movement or (2) a unit having a section or sections which unfold along the entire length of the unit.[28]

The definitions differ in that the regulations governing the Section 3710 guaranty require that the manufactured home be permanently affixed to a lot and classified as real property under state law. To be permanently affixed, the home must be placed on a foundation in a way that satisfies local building codes.[29] This generally means being placed on a permanent foundation, and in some, but not all cases, connection to utilities and ownership of the land, although long-term rental agreements may suffice.[30] Once a home is permanently affixed, it may be titled as real property rather than personal property (as a vehicle is titled). According to the Census Bureau, in 2010, approximately 73% of new manufactured homes were titled as personal property and 22% as real property.[31]

Separate Loan Guaranty for Manufactured Housing, 38 U.S.C. Section 3712

When Congress created the separate loan guaranty for manufactured housing in 1970, it was concerned that returning Vietnam veterans, some without significant financial resources, were unable to afford conventional homes and the costs of financing.[32] The recommendation to include mobile homes as eligible properties for the loan guaranty originated from the President's Committee on the Vietnam Veteran, whose members saw growing construction costs of conventional homes as a barrier to home ownership for veterans.[33] According to the committee, the lower costs of mobile homes represented "an enormous potential in meeting the housing needs of many veterans with low to moderate incomes."[34] It was necessary to add a new manufactured housing portion to the law because, unlike loans for site-built homes, manufactured housing is often financed with "chattel mortgages," which are designed for moveable property and governed by different laws than mortgages for real property.

Manufactured housing loans that are guaranteed through Section 3712 differ from the Section 3710 loan guaranty in that the term of the mortgage is generally shorter depending on the type of manufactured housing,[35] the maximum loan guaranty amount is set differently (see **Table 3**), and fees charged by the VA are less than for conventional housing (see **Table 6**), among other differences. However, as mentioned previously, the VA does not appear to have guaranteed loans pursuant to Section 3712 since FY1996.

Refinancing Loans

Veterans may use the loan guaranty to refinance an existing loan in two different ways: to reduce the interest rate of an existing VA-guaranteed loan (sometimes referred to as an interest rate reduction refinancing loan or IRRRL),[36] or to refinance generally with fewer restrictions. Loans in the latter category are sometimes referred to as "cash out" refinancings because veterans may choose to take out equity as part of the transaction. The ability to refinance a loan on a property owned and occupied by an eligible veteran became part of the loan guaranty law as part of the Veterans' Housing Act of 1970 (P.L. 91-506).[37] Manufactured housing loans became eligible for refinancing as part of the Veterans' Compensation and Program Improvements Amendments of 1984 (P.L. 98-223).

IRRRL: When a veteran refinances a loan that is already guaranteed by the VA as an IRRRL, generally the interest rate on the new loan should be lower than the loan being refinanced.[38] However, a veteran may refinance from an adjustable-rate loan to a fixed-rate loan without the requirement for a lower rate. The amount of the new loan may not exceed the principal balance of the original loan, plus any closing costs, and the term of the new loan cannot exceed the original loan term by more than 10 years.[39] A veteran may also take advantage of energy efficiency improvements as part of an IRRRL, in which case the principal balance of the new loan may be increased by the amount of the improvements.[40] Another aspect of an IRRRL refinancing is that a veteran need not occupy the residence as a home after refinancing as long as it had been occupied as a home prior to refinancing. The limitation on occupancy was removed in 1987 (P.L. 100-198) due to concern that servicemembers who were transferred or stationed elsewhere were unable to take advantage of refinancing.[41] In general, no appraisal and no new underwriting are required for an IRRRL,[42] and, unlike purchase-money VA loans, closing costs may be financed as part of the loan.[43]

"Cash-Out" Refinancing: A veteran may also refinance without the restrictions involved in an IRRRL. The loan or lien being refinanced need not be VA-guaranteed, the new loan does not have to have a lower interest rate, the loan balance on the refinanced loan may be higher than on the original loan, and the veteran may receive cash from the refinancing for any purpose approved by the lender. Property improvements are often undertaken as part of a refinancing.[44] However, there are requirements for cash-out refinancings that are not required for IRRRLs. A veteran must occupy the property as his or her home after the refinancing, and, unlike the IRRRL, an appraisal, credit check, and underwriting are required.[45]

Number and Amount of Loans Guaranteed

VA-guaranteed loans make up a relatively small share of mortgage loans in the United States. According to the 2009 American Housing Survey, approximately 7.6% of primary mortgages outstanding were VA-guaranteed loans.[46] **Table 2** shows the number of loans that have been guaranteed by the VA from FY2000 through FY2011 broken down by purchase and refinance loans, the dollar amount of the loans, and the dollar amount of the portion guaranteed.

Table 2. VA Loans Guaranteed by Fiscal Year, FY2000-FY2011

Fiscal Year	Number of Loans in Year			Volume of Loans Made in Year ($ in billions)		Cumulative Volume of Loans Outstanding[a] ($ in billions)	
	Purchase Loans	Refinance Loans[b]	Total Loans	Amount of Loans	Amount Guaranteed	Amount of Loans	Amount Guaranteed
2000	185,553	13,607	199,160	23.372	7.071	—[c]	—[c]
2001	177,158	72,851	250,009	31.255	9.152	218.455	71.431
2002	176,898	140,353	317,251	40.129	11.667	216.042	69.547
2003	148,810	340,608	489,418	63.255	18.245	213.248	67.654
2004	152,395	183,393	335,788	44.131	12.643	207.374	64.683
2005	119,130	46,724	165,854	24.901	6.808	202.073	62.114
2006	122,604	20,104	142,708	24.635	6.486	203.186	61.277
2007	117,941	15,372	133,313	24.890	6.438	207.644	61.456
2008	142,340	37,330	179,670	36.089	9.236	220.839	63.921
2009	180,896	144,794	325,690	68.201	17.492	183.365	50.368
2010	192,625	121,386	314,011	65.051	16.745	214.726	58.080
2011	186,588	171,006	357,594	74.929	19.318	247.648	66.222

Source: The data on the number and dollar amount of guaranteed loans in a fiscal year are from the Department of Veterans Affairs, *Annual Benefits Reports*. The data on the cumulative volume of loans come from the VA *Performance and Accountability Reports*.

a. The cumulative volume of loans is the total dollar amount of all guaranteed loans that was outstanding at the end of the fiscal year.

b. Refinance loans include interest rate reduction refinancing loans and cash-out or other refinancing transactions.

c. *The FY2000 Performance and Accountability Report* did not provide information about the total loan volume.

During periods where interest rates have fallen, refinance loans make up a greater share of the total VA loans extended. And during the mid-2000s, when housing prices were at their height, the numbers of VA-guaranteed purchase loans were lower than the number entered into at both the beginning and end of the last decade. Among the reasons for this are the fact that looser lending standards on private mortgage loans, particularly subprime loans, might have made them more appealing for veteran borrowers. This may have been particularly true in a climate where the ability to close loans quickly was considered appealing to sellers, and bypassing the VA loan fee was appealing to veteran borrowers.[47] In addition, higher home prices during the mid-2000s could have made it difficult for veterans living in high-cost areas to take advantage of the loan guaranty. Until enactment of legislation in 2008, the VA loan guaranty did not cover properties in high cost areas where the cost exceeded $417,000. (For more information about maximum mortgage limits, see the next section of this report entitled "Amount of Coverage Provided by the Loan Guaranty.")

Amount of Coverage Provided by the Loan Guaranty

While there is technically no limit to the amount that a veteran can borrow and still receive a loan guaranty through the VA, the VA limits the guaranty that it will provide based on the amount of the loan as well as the type of loan (purchase money, refinance, or energy efficiency mortgage). In most cases, the VA guaranty covers at least 25% of the principal balance of a loan. While the VA guaranty does not insure 100% of the loan (as Federal Housing Administration loan insurance does, for example), the guaranty covers what would typically be required as a down payment in a conventional mortgage transaction to avoid the requirement for private mortgage insurance. In cases where the loan guaranty does not cover 25% of the loan amount, a veteran may have to make a down payment.

Freddie Mac Conforming Loan Limit

The conforming loan limit is a ceiling on the value of loans that Freddie Mac, one of the Government Sponsored Enterprises, can purchase from lenders.48 The single-family home loan limit in statute was initially pegged to the FHA insurance limit—$33,750 in 197049— then revised to follow the loan limits for savings and loans.50 However, beginning in 1980 as part of the Housing and Community Development Act (P.L. 96-399), Congress inserted the maximum loan limit directly in the Freddie Mac statute. P.L. 96-399 set the single-family limit at $93,750, and it was to be adjusted administratively each year based on the national average single-family home price.[51] While Congress did not amend the statute to increase the loan limit until 2008, the limit was changed administratively 27 times.[52]

As part of the Housing and Economic Recovery Act of 2008 (P.L. 110-289), Congress amended the Freddie Mac statute to raise the *statutory* conforming loan limit from $93,750 to $417,000, which was the level that had been established administratively for 2006 and 2007. P.L. 110-289 also added a sentence to the statute allowing the limit to increase in high-cost areas where 115% of the median home price exceeds the conforming loan limit. In these high-cost areas, the loan limit may go up to 115% of the area median home price, not to exceed 150% of the loan limit (or as high as $625,500).

Since the enactment of P.L. 110-289, the Freddie Mac statute itself has not been amended, although Congress temporarily raised the loan limits for high-cost areas through September 30, 2011, via several laws. This limit was the lower of 125% of the area median home price or 175% of the Freddie Mac limit (or $729,750).[53] These temporary limits expired at the end of FY2011.

The statute governing the loan guaranty for home purchase sets out four categories of coverage depending on the principal balance of the loan.[54] (For all guaranty amounts, including manufactured housing, refinance loans, and energy efficiency mortgages, see **Table 3**.) In general, the amount of the loan guaranty is based on the amount borrowed by a veteran.

- At loan levels at or below $45,000, the VA guaranties 50% of the loan.
- For loans above $45,000 and up to and including $56,250, the guaranty is $22,500.
- At loan levels above $56,250 and up to and including $144,000, the VA guaranty is the lesser of $36,000 or 40% of the loan.
- For loan levels above $144,000, the maximum loan guaranty is the lesser of the "maximum guaranty amount" or 25% of the loan.
  - The "maximum guaranty amount" is defined in statute as 25% of "the Freddie Mac conforming loan limit limitation determined under section 305(a)(2) of the Federal Home Loan Mortgage Corporation Act."[55] The Freddie Mac statute has most recently set the conforming loan limit at $417,000 for single-family homes (for more information about the Freddie Mac conforming loan limit, see the text box).[56] However, for certain high-cost areas, the loan limit may be as high as 115% of the area median home price, though it may not exceed 150% of the conforming loan limit (or

$625,500).[57] Therefore, depending on where a property is located, the maximum VA loan guaranty is 25% of $625,500, or $156,375. The VA publishes a list of counties where the loan limits exceed $417,000.[58]

Table 3. Limits on the Level of Loan Guaranty

Amount of Loan	Limits on Guaranty
Home Loan Guaranty	
• $45,000 or less	• 50% of the loan amount
• from $45,000 up to and including $56,250	• $22,500
• from $56,250 up to and including $144,000	• Lesser of $36,000 or 40% of the loan amount[a]
• more than $144,000	• Lesser of (1) 25% of the loan amount or (2) 25% of the higher of (a) the Freddie Mac conforming loan limit ($417,000) or (b) 115% of the area median home price, not to exceed 150% of the Freddie Mac conforming loan limit ($625,500).
Refinance: Same as for purchase, but in the case of an interest rate reduction refinancing loan (IRRRL), the guaranty may not exceed the greater of the original loan's guaranty or 25% of the loan.	
Energy Efficiency Improvements: The sum of (1) the guaranty amount without the energy efficiency improvements and (2) the guaranty percentage (from step (1)) multiplied by the portion borrowed for energy efficiency improvements.[b]	
Manufactured Housing Purchase: The lesser of $20,000 or 40% of the loan.	
Manufactured Housing Refinance: If refinancing a VA loan, the guaranty may not exceed the greater of the original loan guaranty or 25% of the refinancing amount.	

Source: 38 U.S.C. §3703(a), §3710(d)-(e), and §3712(a),(c).
a. This effectively means that for loans between $90,000 and $144,000, the maximum guaranty is $36,000.
b. While the Energy Efficiency Improvement guaranty is effectively the same as the guaranty for home purchase, the separate calculations are meant to ensure that the portion of the guaranty related to the improvements are not counted against the veteran's entitlement. 38 U.S.C. §3710(d)(4). See also, *VA Lenders Handbook*, p. 7-20, http://www.benefits.va.gov/WARMS/docs/admin26/pamphlet/pam26_7/ch07.doc.

If the amount of a mortgage exceeds the county Freddie Mac limit (for example, the amount of the mortgage is $500,000 in a county where the loan limit is $417,000), then a veteran may have to make a down payment equal to 25% of the amount over the Freddie Mac limit to qualify for the loan due to secondary market considerations (see the next section of this report entitled "Maximum Loan Amount" for more information about the secondary market). However, the majority of VA-guaranteed loans are made with no down payment (88% of purchase loans in FY2011 had no down payment),[59] so the limits described here will apply to most veteran borrowers.

Maximum Limit for Alaska, Hawaii, U.S. Virgin Islands, and Guam

The maximum single-family guaranty limit for Alaska, Hawaii, the U.S. Virgin Islands, and Guam is higher than in the other states and the District of Columbia due to costs of construction.[60] The Freddie Mac conforming loan limit for these states and territories is 50% higher than the $417,000 limit for the rest of the country, resulting in a current loan limit of $625,500.[61] Further, with the provision allowing the area limit to be increased up to 150% of the conforming loan limit for high-cost areas, it is possible for the loan limit in Alaska, Hawaii, the U.S. Virgin Islands, and Guam to be as high as $938,250 (150% of $625,500), with the VA guaranty set at 25% of this amount, or $234,562. However, in 2012, only Honolulu County exceeded the $625,500 loan limit level.[62]

Loan Limits Prior to January 1, 2012

For a period beginning in 2008 and continuing through December 31, 2011, limits to the VA loan guaranty for loan levels above $144,000 were higher than they are currently. The Veterans' Benefits Improvement Act of 2008 (P.L. 110-389) temporarily increased the "maximum guaranty amount" (it did not make the change in statute). The law set the maximum guaranty amount at the higher of 25% of:

- The Freddie Mac conforming loan limit, or
- 125% of the area median home price, but no higher than 175% of the limit determined under the Freddie Mac statute.

According to guidance issued by the VA,[63] this meant that in high-cost areas where the Freddie Mac statutory loan limit reached $625,500, the VA could guarantee loans up to 175% of $625,500, or $1,094,625.[64] Loan limits in a number of communities exceeded the current maximum level of $625,500 during this time period.[65] The same held true for Alaska, Hawaii, Guam, and the U.S. Virgin Islands. Technically, the maximum loan limit could have been set at $1,641,937.50 (175% of $938,250), though no community in the territories reached this level (and only one, Honolulu County, saw its limit exceed $625,500).

Maximum Loan Amount

Although there is no limit to the amount a veteran may borrow and still participate in the VA loan guaranty program, lenders may be unwilling to extend a loan that exceeds the limit where the VA will guaranty 25% of the loan. VA loans are securitized through the Government National Mortgage Association (Ginnie Mae). Ginnie Mae may secure certain "high balance loans" originated after October 1, 2008—loans where the balance exceeds the conforming loan limit of $417,000 for single-family properties.[66] However, according to the VA, the "rule of thumb" for Ginnie Mae to purchase a VA loan is that at least 25% of the principal balance either be guaranteed and/or covered by a down payment.[67] As a result, the effective maximum loan limit with no down payment corresponds to the "maximum guaranty amount" described in the previous section.

Subsequent Loans: The Veteran's Entitlement

The term "entitlement" is used to refer to the amount of guaranty to which a veteran is entitled under the loan guaranty statute. It is different from the guaranty amount described in the previous section in that it is technically a lifetime limit on the amount of loan insurance coverage for which a veteran may qualify. However, given the broad circumstances under which entitlement may be restored (described below), veterans may use the guaranty for the purchase of more than one home during a lifetime, though not necessarily more than one home at a time.

The statute governing the VA loan guaranty limits a veteran's entitlement to $36,000 or, for loans that exceed $144,000, the "maximum guaranty amount" described in the previous section (under current law, this amount may be no more than $234,562 in high-cost areas).[68] The term "basic entitlement" is sometimes used to refer to entitlement up to $36,000, and the term "bonus entitlement" is used to refer to entitlement that exceeds $36,000. In general, due to the requirement that VA-guaranteed loans be used to purchase properties that a veteran will occupy as his or her home,[69] unused entitlement cannot be used to purchase more than one home at a time.

In addition to being able to put unused entitlement toward a future guaranteed loan, there are instances in which already-used entitlement may be restored so that a veteran may use the maximum available loan guaranty to purchase another home.[70] These circumstances cover most situations where a veteran has ended the previous loan transaction in some way.

- Entitlement is restored where a veteran has disposed of the property (e.g., through sale) or the property has been destroyed through natural disaster, and either (1) the loan is paid off in full; (2) if the VA suffered a loss on the loan, the loss is repaid; or (3) the VA has been released from liability on the loan.
- When one veteran assumes a guaranteed loan from another, entitlement is restored to the original mortgagor.
- In cases of refinancing, entitlement is restored either when a veteran has paid off the original loan prior to entering into a new loan or where proceeds from the refinancing will be used to pay off the original loan.[71]
- Where a veteran has paid off a VA-guaranteed loan, but has not yet sold the property that secured it, the VA may do a one-time restoration of entitlement to be used toward the purchase of another property.[72]

If available entitlement is less than 25% of the loan, then a lender may require a veteran to make a down payment to make up the difference between the loan guaranty and 25% of the loan to meet secondary market requirements.[73]

How the VA Loan Guaranty Differs from FHA Insurance

Both the Federal Housing Administration (FHA) loan insurance program and the VA loan guaranty program provide borrowers with the federal government's promise to reimburse lenders in the event of borrower default on private mortgages. Due to the insurance features of each program, borrowers who might not otherwise have the resources for a conventional mortgage may still be able to purchase a home. Despite similar purposes, however, the programs differ in their specifics. Aside from the requirement that a borrower through the VA meet service requirements, other features such as the amount of coverage, borrower fees, loan processing and underwriting, terms of the loan, etc., vary between the two.

- **Amount of Coverage:** As discussed earlier in the "Amount of Coverage Provided by the Loan Guaranty" section, the VA loan guaranty covers only a portion of the mortgage loan in the event of a borrower's default. Insurance through FHA covers 100% of the loan amount (up to a certain limit).
- **Maximum Loan Amount:** As a practical matter, the maximum loan amount for the VA loan guaranty in certain high-cost areas is $625,500 (see the "Maximum Loan Amount" section of this report). In the case of FHA, the insurance will currently cover loans up to $729,750 in certain high-cost areas.[74]
- **Borrower Fees:** Fees paid by veterans participating in the VA loan guaranty program are paid up front as a percentage of the loan (see **Table 6**), and borrowers do not pay additional annual premiums. Borrowers who go through the FHA program currently pay an up-front fee of 1.75% of the loan amount, and then pay annual premiums of 1.20% or 1.25% of the mortgage balance, depending on the loan-to-value ratio.[75] Beginning on June 11, 2012, FHA borrowers with mortgages greater than $625,500 will pay annual premiums of 1.45% or 1.50%.
- **Down Payment:** Veteran borrowers who participate in the VA loan guaranty program are not required to make a down payment. However, if the loan balance exceeds loan limits, the borrower generally must make up the difference between the guaranty and 25% of the loan amount. In general, borrowers through FHA must make a 3.5% down payment (10% for credit scores ranging from 500 to 579).[76]
- **Fees Charged at Closing:** While both the VA loan guaranty and the FHA insurance program have rules about what lenders may charge borrowers at closing, the VA loan guaranty is more restrictive. VA loan guaranty regulations list services where lenders are allowed to charge itemized fees to borrowers (such as appraisal, recording, and credit report fees),[77] and any other fees must be recouped through a flat fee not to exceed 1% of the loan, limiting such charges as application fees, document preparation, interest rate lock-in fees, and charges from mortgage brokers.[78] FHA rules are more general,

specifying that lenders "may only collect fair, reasonable, and customary fees and charges" from borrowers.[79]

- **Minimum Credit Score:** The VA loan guaranty does not require a specific credit score from a borrower, while FHA requires a credit score of at least 500.[80]

- **Appraisal:** Appraisers for properties that are to be guaranteed through the VA loan guaranty program must go through a separate VA certification procedure, and they are chosen by the VA rather than lenders.[81] The statute requires the VA to review appraisals prior to loan closings, although the VA has a program in place to allow lenders to process appraisals after application and training.[82] FHA does not have similar policies regarding appraisers, and they may be selected by lenders.

In addition, for a number of years, veterans were given special terms when entering into FHA loans. The Housing and Urban Development Act of 1965 (P.L. 89-117) first allowed veterans to enter into FHA loans with slightly higher maximum mortgages compared to nonveteran borrowers, and it also exempted them from what was then a 3% cash down payment requirement on the first $15,000 of the loan. Over time, some of the specifics of the maximum mortgage and down payment requirements have changed, but veterans still retained favorable levels compared to nonveterans. In 2002, the FHA Downpayment Simplification Act (P.L. 107-326) removed statutory language that allowed for higher maximum mortgages for veteran borrowers.[83] And when the Housing and Economic Recovery Act of 2008 (P.L. 110-289) was enacted, it eliminated the provision exempting veterans from the requirement of what had previously been a 3% down payment in cash or its equivalent.[84]

DIRECT VA LOANS

In addition to the VA loan guaranty program, through which the VA insures loans made to veterans by private lenders, there are several circumstances under which the VA makes loans directly to veterans, as well as occasionally to nonveterans. The direct loans through the VA can be put into two broad categories. The first category involves loans that are targeted to specific veteran populations: one program was created to address the needs of rural veterans, but has evolved to serve veterans with certain disabilities, and the other program is designed for Native American veterans. The second category involves loans made as the result of borrower default on guaranteed loans—these are referred to as "acquired loans" and "vendee loans."

The Original Direct Loan for Veterans in Rural Areas, Now Limited to Veterans with Disabilities

The VA first made direct housing loans available to veterans who were unable to obtain mortgages through private lenders and were therefore unable to participate in the loan guaranty program. The direct loan portion of the program was enacted as part of the Housing Act of 1950 (P.L. 81-475), and was meant to be a "last resort" where private financing was not available to veterans.[85] The enacting legislation did not specify that the program was directed to veterans in rural areas, but about eight years later, in 1958, Congress changed the law to apply specifically to veterans living in rural areas and small towns as part of P.L. 85-857.[86] The law provided that the VA Secretary would designate an area without private loan options for veterans as a "housing credit shortage area" and make loans to veterans at a rate not exceeding the rate set for guaranteed loans at a maximum principal balance (at the time the law was enacted) of $13,500. In the Veterans' Housing Act of 1970 (P.L. 91-506), Congress made direct loans available to veterans who qualified for Specially Adapted Housing grants for veterans with certain disabilities, who it recognized might also have difficulty obtaining credit for home purchases.[87]

The VA direct loan program continues to exist today, but in limited form.[88] A 1980 review of the direct loan program found that 98% of veterans in rural areas received loans from private lenders, and only 2% received VA direct loans.[89] As a result of the increased availability of private loan funds in rural areas, beginning in the FY1981 Department of Housing and Urban Development-Independent Agencies Appropriation Act (P.L. 96-526), Congress specified that VA direct loans be made only for veterans with disabilities through the Specially Adapted Housing Program (described in a later section of this report entitled "The Specially Adapted Housing Program"). Congress has continued to include similar language in subsequent appropriations acts.[90] Currently, direct loans are limited to $500,000 in obligations for Specially Adapted Housing loans of not more than $33,000 apiece.[91] Interest rates on the loans are to be determined by the VA Secretary, and veterans are eligible as long as they qualify for the loan guaranty program.

Direct Loans for Native American Veterans (Including Guam, American Samoa, and CNMI)

While the VA loan guaranty program is available to Native American veterans,[92] due in part to certain tribal land ownership issues, Congress enacted a direct loan program specifically to provide mortgage assistance for Native American veterans. The direct loan program may also be used by veteran borrowers who are Native Hawaiians, Alaska Natives, and those who are native to American Samoa, Guam, and the Commonwealth of the Northern Mariana Islands (CNMI).[93]

Prior to enactment of the direct loan program for Native American veterans, VA housing assistance to Native American veterans was minimal. In fact, the Advisory Committee on Native American Veterans had been unable to find a single instance of a Native American veteran benefitting from the loan guaranty program.[94] While factors such as poverty and unemployment among Native American veterans may have contributed to their lack of participation, the unique nature of tribal land also presented obstacles to private lenders entering into mortgages. Much of tribal land is held in trust by the federal government, either for a tribe or for individual Native Americans (the latter situation is sometimes referred to as an allotment). Of the approximately 56 million acres of trust land, 45 million are held in trust for tribes and 11 million for individuals.[95] In the case of tribal trust land, the land may be assigned or leased to individual tribal members. However, in neither case (tribal or individual trust) may the land be encumbered or transferred without federal government approval.[96] Lenders could be reluctant to enter into mortgage arrangements where they would be unable to have the land transferred to them in the event of a veteran's default.[97]

Similar issues apply to residents of American Samoa and CNMI, where land ownership is restricted. In American Samoa, approximately 90% of land is communally held,[98] it may not be transferred without government approval, and it may not be transferred to anyone who is "less than one half Samoan."[99] The CNMI Constitution restricts land ownership and long-term interests (such as leases) to those of Northern Marianan descent.[100] As with tribal land, a private lender may not be willing to extend a loan where transfer of the land in the event of default would violate territorial law. Guam does not have these restricted land ownership issues.

After finding that only 15 of 24,000 veterans living on trust land had participated in any sort of housing benefit—all of whom received the Specially Adapted Housing benefit and none the loan guaranty—Congress initially enacted a demonstration program to make loans to Native American veterans that was included in the Veterans Home Loan Program Amendments of 1992 (P.L. 102547).[101] The program was made permanent as part of the Veterans' Housing Opportunity and Benefits Improvement Act of 2006 (P.L. 109-233). In order to participate in the VA direct loan program, and circumvent the issues of land ownership, a tribe must enter into a memorandum of understanding (MOU) with the VA to provide avenues for addressing default and foreclosure.

Typically individuals enter into long-term leases for use of trust land. The MOU requires that a participating tribe set up a process through which a veteran borrower's leasehold interest in a property can be transferred to a lender, whether private or government, or their assignee in the event of default.[102] The tribe must also establish a procedure for evicting and foreclosing on the veteran's interest in the land and property.

As of FY2011, the VA had entered into MOUs with 83 tribes or Pacific Island territories.[103] Through FY2011, the VA had entered into 869 loans through the direct loan program, 41 of which were made in that year.[104] The Direct Loan program for Native American veterans has had much of its participation in Hawaii and the territories. Prior to the program being made permanent in 2006, the VA noted in hearing testimony that the program was most successful in American Samoa, Guam, CNMI, and Hawaii, with 90% of loans at the time made in American Samoa and Hawaii.[105] Reasons behind the lack of lending to Native American veterans were thought to include low income, lack of infrastructure, and poor credit.[106] As of calendar year 2011, 90% of loans were still made in American Samoa and Hawaii.[107]

Direct Loans Resulting from Borrower Delinquency or Default (Acquired and Vendee Loans)

The VA may also enter into a direct loan arrangement in two situations involving a veteran's delinquency and/or default on a guaranteed loan.

- **Acquired Loans:** In situations where a veteran borrower with a guaranteed loan has difficulty making payments, the VA may purchase the loan from the lender (or current servicer) and continue to hold and service the loan.[108]
- **Vendee Loans:** In cases where a veteran defaults on a guaranteed loan and the lender forecloses, the VA often acquires the property

from the servicer and then resells it. As part of the resale, the VA may enter into a direct loan with a purchaser of the home, whether or not the purchaser is a veteran. The VA briefly suspended the vendee loan program in 2003, but Congress reinstated it as part of the Veterans Benefits Act (P.L. 108-183). The law also amended the statute to require that, of the properties acquired and sold by the VA as the result of veteran default, between 50% and 85% are to be financed by the VA as part of their purchase.[109]

Generally, the VA has had the authority to bundle and sell pools of vendee loans.[110] The loans are sold to a trust, which in turn issues certificates that are backed by the mortgages and sold to investors. The VA guarantees that investors in the certificates will receive "full and timely" payments of principal and interest from the loans as well as against losses at foreclosure.[111] The bundled loans appear in the VA budget as "Guaranteed Loan Sales Securities." However, the authority to bundle and sell the loans expired on December 31, 2011. The VA may still sell loans individually.[112]

Table 4. Direct Loans for Native American Veterans,
FY2000-FY2011

Fiscal Year	Number of Loans	Amount of Loans Made During the Year ($ in millions)
2000	21	1.871
2001	20	1.544
2002	62	5.620
2003	120	10.637
2004	56	4.924
2005	38	3.266
2006	30	4.957
2007	53	7.378
2008	42	8.288
2009	99	15.725
2010	103	15.835
2011	41	7.492

Source: U.S. Department of Veterans Affairs, *Annual Benefits Reports*, FY2000 to FY2011.

Table 5. Guaranteed Loans Acquired by VA, Vendee Loans Extended, and Direct Loans Sold

Fiscal Year	Loans Acquired and Serviced by VA	Vendee Loans Entered Into by VA as Part of Property Sale	Vendee Loans Sold by VA
1998	2,001	15,856	—[a]
1999	1,573	16,871	11,952
2000	4,256	13,698	18,434
2001	2,775	11,186	9,282
2002	2,693	8,786	11,714
2003	1,740	4,621	3,333
2004	1,171	3	3,397
2005	1,161	1,419	0
2006	1,150	788	0
2007	642	501	0
2008	386	626	2,532
2009	81	435	0
2010	36	1,081	2,190
2011	92	4,660	1,725

Source: VA Budget Justifications for Veterans Benefits Programs, FY2000-FY2013.
a. The number of vendee loans for FY1998 was not available.

The number of loans acquired by the VA, vendee loans entered into, and sales of vendee loans in a given year depend on borrower defaults, purchaser interest in foreclosed VA homes, and investor interest in VA securities. **Table 5** shows the number of acquired loans, vendee loans entered into, and vendee loans sold from FY1998 through FY2011. As a result of the vendee loan program suspension in 2003, the number of vendee loans sold decreased during the following years and has only recently begun to pick up again. This has also resulted in the sale of fewer vendee loans. In addition, the number of VA acquired loans has fallen in recent years. According to the VA, there have been fewer acquired loans since the 1990s and early 2000s because both the VA and loan servicers focused efforts on loan modification and other options to help borrowers keep their homes, reducing the need for the VA to acquire loans.[113] Efforts particularly increased in 2008 and thereafter, when the VA offered new incentives for servicers to work with borrowers (see the section of this report "Options to Prevent Foreclosure").

Federal Credit Reform Act of 1990

The FCRA (P.L. 101-508[114]) changed the way in which the federal government budgets for loan and loan guaranty programs like those administered by the VA. Prior to the FCRA, if a federal agency extended direct loans to borrowers in a given fiscal year, the disbursement of the principal balance of the loans was recorded as an outlay in that year, and the budget did not account for the fact that the government would recoup principal and interest payments in future years. Loan guarantees, by contrast, could appear costless in the early years, or even income-generating if fees were collected, but did not reflect potential costs due to defaulted loans in the future.

Beginning in 1992, the FCRA required agency budgets to reflect the *net present value* of outflows and inflows of a loan over its lifetime. The estimated cash inflows and outflows of a program are discounted to the present fiscal year using a discount rate. A credit subsidy in the form of an appropriation from the federal government may be required to support loan programs when the net present value is positive.

Due to the uncertainty involved in making the net present value estimates, OMB and federal agencies re-estimate the credit subsidy each year to determine the actual subsidy required. Additional funding in subsequent years that may be required due to underestimates of the subsidy comes from "permanent indefinite authority" provided through the FCRA rather than annual discretionary appropriations.

Within their budgets, federal agencies account for loans entered into prior to 1992 separately, in a liquidating account.

FUNDING FOR THE VA DIRECT AND GUARANTEED LOAN PROGRAMS

Both the VA direct loan and loan guaranty programs are funded through several sources. These sources include congressional appropriations, fees paid by borrowers, proceeds from the rental or sale of foreclosed properties, collection of principal and interest payments made by borrowers, and any penalties paid by lenders.[115] An important aspect of understanding how VA loans are funded, apart from the sources of funding, is how loans are accounted for in the federal budget.

In most federally funded *grant* programs, the cost to the federal budget is the amount appropriated, and federal involvement in funding generally ends after the outlay of funds. By contrast, the cost of *loan* programs may involve both an up-front outlay of funds as well as the recoupment of costs through payments of principal and interest, and/or collection of fees and penalties, over the lifetime of the loans. Loan programs may also suffer losses in subsequent years through defaults or lower-than-expected collection of fees. As a result, it is not always possible to capture the budgetary effects of loans in one particular year. Current government practice, instituted in 1992, is to determine the *net present value* of loans over their lifetime and to record this amount in the budget in the year the loans are extended. (See the text box for an explanation of the law implementing this budget process.)

The concept of net present value is helpful both in understanding how funds are appropriated for VA loans and in reading VA budget documents. The federal funding process is described briefly in the following subsection of this report, "The VA Budget and Congressional Appropriations for VA Loan Programs." The two subsequent subsections describe loan fees paid by borrowers, and funds obtained through loan payments and property sales.

Sources of Funding for Loan Programs

The VA Budget and Congressional Appropriations for VA Loan Programs

The VA direct and guaranteed loan programs receive both discretionary and mandatory appropriations from Congress. The discretionary funds pay for the administrative expenses of the VA loan programs. The mandatory funding supports the loans themselves, and typically appears in appropriations laws as "such sums as necessary."

Mandatory funding for the loan guaranty and direct loan programs is expressed as a percentage of the total loan volume. This is sometimes referred to as the "subsidy rate"; each year the estimated subsidy rate appears in the President's Budget Appendix for the Department of Veterans Affairs. The estimated subsidy rate of loans guaranteed or made in a given fiscal year is based on the net present value of expected expenses in the event of borrower defaults as well as expected income through fees and other sources. If the estimated present value of payments by the VA for a cohort of loans guaranteed or extended in a given fiscal year exceeds the estimated present value of fees paid by borrowers, recoveries, and other collections, then the subsidy rate is positive (i.e., the government subsidizes the loan program), and the program receives mandatory funding. If the net present value of cash flows for a cohort of loans is expected to result in a surplus of funds (more taken in than paid out), then the subsidy rate is negative (i.e., the program has excess revenue that is returned to Treasury).

As part of the annual budget process, the VA estimates individual subsidy rates for each of the four types of loans either made directly by the VA or guaranteed by the VA. The four programs for which the VA estimates subsidy rates are guaranteed loans, guaranteed loan sale securities, acquired loans, and vendee loans. The initial estimated subsidy rate for each of these programs for a given fiscal year represents the net present value for that year's cohort of loans. However, the initial estimated subsidy rate may differ from the actual subsidy rate for the cohort of loans over their lifetime. Projecting the net present value of cash flows is uncertain, so subsidy reestimates are made by the VA each year, and additional mandatory funding is permanently available by the FCRA to cover any shortfalls.[116] Factors that can affect the subsidy rate (and resulting mandatory appropriation) include changes in the interest rate used to determine the present value of future funding streams, revisions in estimates of borrower default or prepayment rates, the outcomes of property management decisions, and changes in the amount of fees actually paid by borrowers (compared to what was expected). Due to reestimates, a negative subsidy rate calculated in one year may be recalculated as positive in a subsequent year, resulting in an increased amount of mandatory funding needed for a loan program. Or, if the subsidy rate is recalculated as negative, funds are returned to Treasury.

Appropriations for VA direct and guaranteed loans are captured in one "on-budget" account, called the Veterans Housing Benefit Program Fund, sometimes referred to as the program account.[117] (Note that direct loans for Native American veterans are funded separately.) In addition, several separate, off-budget accounts reflect inflows and outflows for direct and guaranteed loan cohorts, depending on when the loans were extended. Funds for direct and guaranteed loans made prior to 1992 are shown in a housing liquidating account, and funds for loans extended after 1992 are shown in direct and guaranteed loan financing accounts. The multiple accounts may be cause for confusion, so it is useful to keep in mind that appropriations appear in the Veterans Housing Benefit Program Fund, while the financing and liquidating accounts reflect the specific income and expenses associated with particular loan cohorts.

Fees from Borrowers

The costs of the VA direct and loan guaranty programs are supported, in part, by fees paid by the borrowers. The amount of a borrower's fee is based on the amount of down payment, if any; whether the loan is extended through the loan guaranty or direct loan program; whether the borrower had active duty service or was a reservist; when the loan closed; whether the loan is purchase money or a refinance; whether the borrower is accessing the guaranty for the first time or entering into a subsequent loan; and whether the property is purchased under the manufactured housing portion of the loan guaranty statute.[118] (See **Table 6.**) Fees may be waived for veterans receiving compensation for a service-connected disability or for the surviving spouse of a servicemember who died of a service-connected disability.[119] Veterans may finance the fees as part of the loan, and the guaranty is based on the loan amount, including the fees.[120]

Veterans were not always charged fees as part of the loan guaranty transaction and, in general, fees were not required prior to 1982.[121] When the loan guaranty program was created, it was considered a benefit or entitlement for veterans. However, in 1982, the VA administrator wrote a letter to the Speaker of the House, together with draft legislation, suggesting that the VA require veterans to pay a 0.5% fee on the principal balance of each loan.[122] The letter expressed concern regarding the "costs to the taxpayers of operating the program," and noted that "paying claims on the approximately 3.7 percent of the loans resulting in foreclosure are significant."[123] Despite objections from veterans groups,[124] Congress instituted the fee as part of the Omnibus Budget Reconciliation Act of 1982 (P.L. 97-253). The fee was to be in effect for transactions entered into from FY1983 through FY1985, with an exemption for veterans with service-connected disabilities. Congress continued the fee beyond FY1985, and after the fee was raised to 1% as part of the Deficit Reduction Act of 1984 (P.L. 98-369), Congress began to institute the more complicated fee schedule that exists today, with fees varying based on amount of down payment and whether the veteran received a loan guaranty or direct loan (Veterans' Benefits Amendments of 1989, P.L. 101-237).

The most recent changes to borrowers' fees occurred as part of P.L. 112-56, which was enacted on November 21, 2011. Prior to the enactment of P.L. 112-56, fees for both active duty and reserve veterans entering into purchase money guaranteed loans were scheduled to be reduced starting on October 1, 2011, pursuant to the Veterans Benefits Act of 2003 (P.L. 108-183). However, the Veterans Health Care Facilities Capital Improvement Act of 2011 (P.L. 112-37), enacted on October 5, 2011, initially extended the existing, higher fees implemented in P.L. 108-183 through November 18, 2011. Then, P.L. 112-56 further extended existing fees through October 1, 2016.[125]

The fees in P.L. 112-56 took effect on the date of enactment. For loans that closed from October 1 through October 5, and from November 18 through November 21, the VA issued guidance stating that the lower fees in P.L. 108-183 applied.[126]

Table 6. Current Loan Guaranty Fees Effective Until October 1, 2016

Loan Type	Down Payment	First Loan or Subsequent	Fee as % of Loan Amount	
			Active Duty	Reservist
Loan to Purchase or Construct Dwelling (38 U.S.C. §3710(a))	Less than 5%	First	2.15%	2.40%
	Less than 5%	Subsequent	3.30%	3.30%
	5%-10%	First or Subsequent	1.50%	1.75%
	10% or more	First	1.25%	1.50%
Cash-Out Refinancing Loan (38 U.S.C. §3710)	NA	First	2.15%	2.40%
	NA	Subsequent	3.30%	3.30%
Manufactured Housing Loan to Purchase or Construct or for Cash- Out Refinancing (38 U.S.C. §3712)	Any	Either	1.00%	1.00%
Interest Rate Reduction Refinancing Loan (38 U.S.C. §3710, §3712, and §3762)	NA	Either	0.50%	0.50%
Direct Loan for Specially Adapted Housing (38 U.S.C. §3711)	Any	Either	1.00%	1.00%
Direct Loans for Native American Veterans to Purchase or Construct (38 U.S.C. §3762)	Any	Either	1.25%	1.25%
Assumption of Guaranteed Loan (38 U.S.C. §3714)	Any	Either	0.50%	0.50%
Vendee Loan (38 U.S.C. §3733(a))	Any	Either	2.25%	2.25%

Source: 38 U.S.C. §3729 as amended by P.L. 112-26 and P.L. 112-56 and the *VA Lenders Handbook*, p. 8-21.

Collection of Loan Payments and Property Sales

In its direct loan portfolio, the VA owns some loans on which it collects principal and interest payments (acquired loans), and it also sells properties that it has acquired through foreclosure and enters into direct loans with the borrowers (vendee loans). In addition, until the authority expired at the end of 2011, the VA could pool and sell loans to investors. Each of these transactions results in income to the VA, although the income may not be sufficient to counteract losses. For example, because the VA guarantees payment of principal and interest on the loans that it sells, borrower default may result in greater outflows than inflows.

THE SPECIALLY ADAPTED HOUSING PROGRAM

The Specially Adapted Housing Program provides grants to veterans and servicemembers with certain service-connected disabilities to assist them in purchasing or remodeling homes to fit their needs.[127] While Specially Adapted Housing loans are available (see discussion in the "The Original Direct Loan for Veterans in Rural Areas, Now Limited to Veterans with Disabilities" section of this report), the majority of funds are distributed as grants that veterans and servicemembers need not pay back.

The Specially Adapted Housing Program, which was introduced in 1948 in P.L. 80-702, initially targeted veterans with a total service-connected disability causing paralysis in the legs or lower body. Over the years, Congress amended the law to expand the range of disabilities eligible for assistance, to make family members' homes eligible for adaptation (P.L. 109-233), to include active duty servicemembers with service-connected disabilities (P.L. 110-289), to expand benefits to individuals residing outside the United States (P.L. 110-289), and to include loans as well as grants (P.L. 96-526).

Within the Specially Adapted Housing Program are two grant programs for veterans and active duty servicemembers, which are discussed in separate subsections, below.[128] The first, sometimes referred to as the Specially Adapted Housing Grant (or §2101(a) grant, after the section of the U.S. Code), is targeted to veterans with mobility impairments, while the second, sometimes referred to as the Special Housing Adaptation Grant (or §2101(b) grant) assists veterans who are blind or who have lost the use of their hands. The grant limits for the first category of adapted housing are higher than for the second, and both types of adapted housing are available to veterans with severe burn injuries.

Specially Adapted Housing Grants, 38 U.S.C. Section 2101(a)

The original law authorizing the Specially Adapted Housing Program was enacted to assist veterans who had lost use of their legs due to either spinal cord disease or injury. The law originally provided for grants of up to $10,000 for veterans to build homes with features adapted to their disabilities, to purchase homes that were already adapted, or to purchase homes without adaptations and then modify them. Since the program was introduced, the grant limit has increased (see "Grant Limits") and the original disability requirement was modified and expanded to include veterans and servicemembers with a broader range of mobility impairments:

- Those who have lost the use of both lower extremities and require the aid of braces, crutches, canes, or a wheelchair (P.L. 86-239).
- Veterans and servicemembers who are blind and have lost the use of at least one lower extremity requiring braces, crutches, canes, or a wheelchair for mobility (P.L. 86-239).
- Veterans and servicemembers who have lost the use of a lower extremity, together with an organic disease or injury requiring use of a cane, crutches, braces, or wheelchair (P.L. 91-22).
- Those who have lost the use of a lower extremity together with one of two conditions that requires use of a cane, crutches, braces, or wheelchair:
  - the loss or loss of use of an upper extremity, or
  - residuals of an organic disease or injury (P.L. 95-117);
- Veterans and servicemembers who have lost the use of both upper extremities such that they cannot use their arms at or above the elbows (P.L. 108-454).
- Veterans and servicemembers with severe burn injuries (P.L. 110-289). VA regulations define this to mean "full thickness or subdermal burns" reducingmobility in two or more extremities or at least one extremity and the trunk of the body.[129]

Special Housing Adaptation Grants, 38 U.S.C. Section 2101(b)

In the Veterans' Disability Compensation and Housing Benefits Amendments of 1980 (P.L. 96-385), Congress expanded the Specially Adapted Housing Program to include veterans who may need to modify their homes, but not to the degree required for veterans eligible for the Section 2101(a) grant. This portion of the program is sometimes referred to as the "Special Housing Adaptation Grant."

The impetus to expand the Specially Adapted Housing Program grew out of the concern that the needs of totally blind veterans were not being met.[130] Unless blind veterans were also without use of a lower extremity, they did not qualify for the Specially Adapted Housing Program, and while they could receive home modifications through VA's home health program, the modifications were limited to $2,500. Congress was concerned that the health program's home modifications were not sufficient to serve veterans who were blind, so it requested a study of the needs of blind veterans as part of P.L. 96-22, the Veterans' Health Care Amendments of 1979.[131] While the report did not contain definitive data about the modification needs of blind veterans, the same year that the report was released, Congress enacted the Veterans' Disability Compensation and Housing and Housing Benefits Amendments of 1980 (P.L. 96-385), which created a new category in the Specially Adapted Housing Program for veterans who were totally blind, as well as those who had lost use of both hands. The Senate Veterans' Affairs Committee noted that home adaptation needs for these veterans might not be as extensive as those with mobility issues, and they did not warrant grant amounts at the same level.[132] At the time the law was enacted, Specially Adapted Housing Grants were limited to $30,000; the portion of the program to assist blind veterans and those without use of their hands was limited to $5,000 in 1980.

Since enactment, the Special Housing Adaptation Grant has been expanded to include veterans with severe burn injuries (P.L. 110-289). According to VA regulations, a veteran qualifies for the grant if (1) the burns are considered "deep partial thickness burns" and result in limitation in motion of two or more extremities or at least one extremity and the trunk of the body, (2) the burns are considered "full thickness or subdermal burns" and result in limitation in motion of one or more extremities or the trunk of the body, or (3) the veteran has residuals of an inhalation injury.[133]

Use of Grants to Modify the Home of a Family Member

The law provides that veterans may use the Special Housing Adaptation grant (§2101(b)) to modify homes of family members in cases where a veteran or servicemember plans to continue living there. In addition, a separate provision in the law, enacted in 2006, specifically provides the authority to give these grants to veterans or servicemembers living *temporarily* in the homes of family members, whether the individual meets disability requirements for Section 2101(a) or Section 2101(b). This is sometimes referred to as the Temporary Residence Adaptation (TRA) grant.

The TRA grant was set up as a five-year pilot program and enacted as part of the Veterans' Housing Opportunity and Benefits Improvement Act of 2006 (P.L. 109-233). There was concern that many injured veterans returning from Operation Iraqi Freedom and Operation Enduring Freedom did not have homes of their own and were instead returning to family members' homes.[134] The grants for veterans and servicemembers living temporarily in the homes of family members allow individuals to access a portion of the full grant to which they are entitled. The program is authorized through December 31, 2012 (P.L. 112-37).

Grant Limits

When the Specially Adapted Housing and Special Housing Adaptation grant programs were created, the Section 2101(a) grant had a limit of $10,000, while the Section 2101(b) limit was set at $5,000. Over the years, Congress increased the limits, most recently to $60,000 and $12,000, respectively. In addition, the Housing and Economic Recovery Act of 2008 (P.L. 110-289) provided that the VA Secretary shall annually adjust the levels based on a residential home cost-of-construction index, to be established by the Secretary.[135] Most recently, in 2010, as a result of this index adjustment, the levels were set at $63,780 for Section 2101(a) grants and $12,756 for Section 2101(b) grants. The VA maintained the same grant limits for FY2011 and FY2012.[136] The limits for the TRA grants—$14,000 for Section 2101(a)-eligible recipients and $2,000 for Section 2101(b)-eligible recipients—have not changed since the pilot program was enacted.

A veteran may qualify for more than one housing grant under the Specially Adapted Housing Program. For example, a veteran or servicemember could make some improvements to his or her home using a Section 2101(a) grant, and receive an additional grant later, as long as the total of all grants did not exceed the $63,780 cap. However, grants used in one component of the program count against the maximum grant for another component. For example, if a veteran received a TRA grant to improve the home of a parent with whom he was residing temporarily, the amount of that grant would reduce the total Section 2101(a) grant he would be eligible to receive if he later purchased his own home. Similarly, a veteran or servicemember who receives a Section 2101(b) grant, and who later qualifies for a Section 2101(a) grant, would have the maximum grant reduced by the amount already used.

The number and amount of Section 2101(a) and Section 2101(b) grants made in recent years are in **Table 8**, below. Funding for the Specially Adapted Housing Program is mandatory funding provided through the Readjustment Benefits portion of the Veterans Benefits Administration budget. Grants are available to veterans and servicemembers based on eligibility rather than amounts appropriated. The appropriation does not contain a specific allocation for Specially Adapted Housing grants. Instead, the VA estimates the amount that will be obligated as part of its Congressional Budget Justifications, which is subsumed in the total for Readjustment Benefits.

The number and dollar amount of Specially Adapted Housing (§2101(a)) grants nearly doubled from FY2007 to FY2008, and have remained higher than in previous years since that time. In addition to an increase in need due to veterans returning from the wars in Iraq and Afghanistan, VA cited broadened eligibility as a factor contributing to the increases in grants distributed.[137] The Housing and Economic Recovery Act of 2008 (P.L. 110-289) made a number of changes to the grants, among them making active duty servicemembers eligible for the grants, including severe burn injuries as an eligible disability, and increasing maximum grants from $50,000 to $60,000 for Section 2101(a) grants, and from $10,000 to $12,000 for Section 2101(b) grants. The increases applied to veterans who had previously received grant assistance.

Table 7. Specially Adapted Housing Grant Limits, 2012

Location	§2101(a) Specially Adapted Housing Grant	§2101(b) Special Housing Adaptation Grant
Veteran's or Servicemember's Own Home	$63,780	$12,756
Family Member's Home (indefinite)	NA	$12,756
Family Member's Home (temporary)	$14,000	$2,000

Source: 38 U.S.C. §2102, 38 U.S.C. §2102A, and Department of Veterans Affairs, "VA Announces Amounts of Assistance for Veterans Under the VA Specially Adapted Housing Program for Fiscal Year 2012."

Table 8. Specially Adapted Housing and Special Housing Adaptation Grants FY2000-FY2011

Fiscal Year	Specially Adapted Housing Grants		Special Housing Adaptation Grants	
	Number of Grants	Amount of Grants in Year ($ in millions)	Number of Grants	Amount of Grants in Year ($ in millions)
2000	509	21.308	65	0.507
2001	456	19.600	49	0.510
2002	475	23.365	56	0.459
2003	435	20.467	58	0.518
2004	450	22.008	51	0.484
2005	526	25.742	61	0.580
2006	503	24.176	45	0.412
2007	585	24.235	68	0.675
2008	1,058	36.000	70	0.760
2009	1,189	51.547	81	0.750
2010	1,421	64.972	128	1.165
2011	1,135	54.833	100	0.897

Source: U.S. Department of Veterans Affairs, *Annual Benefits Reports*, FY1999-FY2011, available at http://www.vba.va.gov/REPORTS/abr/index.asp.

Special Considerations on Trust Lands

In order to qualify for the maximum available assistance through the Section 2101(a) grant, a veteran or servicemember must have an ownership interest in the property being purchased or modified.[138] Until recently, the allowable forms of ownership were somewhat limited. An ownership interest, defined in regulation, included a fee simple interest, a lease or interest in a cooperative of at least 50 years, or a life estate through a revocable trust. As mentioned in the section about the VA direct loan program, individuals living on Native American trust land may not have a traditional interest in property, and individuals living in American Samoa and the Commonwealth of the Northern Mariana Islands may not own property unless they meet nativity requirements.

In 2010, the VA, recognizing the limitations facing veterans or servicemembers living on trust land or in the territories, issued a final rule that updated the regulations defining an ownership interest (among other changes).[139] Individuals may now qualify for the 2101(a) grant if they have a life estate (without the limitation of a revocable trust), the functional equivalent of a life estate (such as a long-term lease or land installment contract), a lease pursuant to a memorandum of understanding between a tribe and the VA, or a beneficial interest in property located outside of the United States, defined as "an interest deemed by the Secretary as one that provides (or will provide) an eligible individual a meaningful right to occupy a housing unit as a residence."[140]

Veterans or servicemembers using the Section 2101(b) grants may qualify for the full grant if they live in the home of a family member, so ownership interests may not be as important. For example, a veteran who does not meet the nativity requirements for property ownership in the territories may have a spouse who does.

VA ACTIONS IN EVENT OF DELINQUENCY, DEFAULT, AND FORECLOSURE

Delinquencies and foreclosures for all categories of loans, including VA-guaranteed loans, have increased in recent years. Beginning about the same time that the country entered recession (December 2007)[141], the housing market began to experience difficulties, with the percentage of all loans past due and the percentage of loans in foreclosure both beginning to grow. In the first quarter of 2007, the overall foreclosure rate was 1.28%; by the fourth quarter of 2011, the rate was 4.38%.[142] During the same period, the percentage of loans 90 days or more past due increased from 0.98% to 3.11%. The peak for loans 90 days or more past due was 5.02% in the first quarter of 2010, and foreclosures reached 4.64% in the fourth quarter of 2010.

While foreclosures for all categories of loans have increased since the beginning of the recession, the foreclosure and delinquency rates for VA-guaranteed loans have been lower than the rates for FHA loans, as well as lower than the overall rates.[143] During the period from the first quarter of 2007 through the fourth quarter of 2011, the foreclosure rate for VA-guaranteed loans increased from 1.05% to 2.37%, and for FHA loans from 2.19% to 3.54%.[144] The rate for loans 90 days or more past due for VA loans increased from 1.52% to 2.26%, and for FHA loans from 3.34% to 5.10%. Foreclosure and delinquency rates for VA loans have not always been lower than FHA loans or loans in general.[145] The VA has suggested a number of factors that could contribute to the recently exhibited lower default rates, including underwriting practices, oversight of lenders, and a robust default servicing program where the VA gets directly involved with borrowers and servicers, if necessary.[146] The increased popularity of subprime loans leading up to the recession may also have contributed to comparably lower rates for VA loans by moving veterans away from VA loans.

Options to Prevent Foreclosure

A number of options may exist for veterans who entered into mortgages through the VA Loan Guaranty Program and find themselves facing delinquency or foreclosure.

Servicer Workouts: One way in which the VA Loan Guaranty Program attempts to prevent properties from going to foreclosure is to encourage servicers to work out agreements with borrowers. In cases where veterans are delinquent on VA-guaranteed loans, the VA may make incentive payments to servicers that are able to work out arrangements with borrowers to prevent foreclosure.[147] These arrangements, or loss mitigation efforts, include repayment plans, forbearance agreements, loan modifications, sales for less than the amount owed ("compromise sales"), or deeds in lieu of foreclosure. Most of these efforts were introduced when VA revised its regulations in 2008.[148] Under existing VA regulations, a lender may enter into a loan modification with a borrower without prior VA approval in circumstances where the borrower is in default, the reasons for loan default have been resolved and are not expected to recur, the borrower is a "reasonable" credit risk, at least 12 payments have been made since the loan closed, and a loan modification would reinstate the loan.[149] On February 7, 2011, the VA published an interim final rule in the Federal Register modifying these regulations to further help encourage modifications.[150] In cases where the conditions listed above have not been met, lenders will be able to request approval from the VA to modify loans nonetheless. In addition, maximum interest rates for modified loans will be tied to the Freddie Mac weekly maximum interest rate (to make it easier to re-pool and securitize modified loans with loans having similar interest rates), and legal fees and foreclosure costs can now be added to the principal balance of a modified loan.

VA Servicing: The VA may intervene to assist with loss mitigation efforts if the servicer has been unwilling or unable to work with the borrower, or if the VA has determined that the loan servicing is inadequate.[151] If loss mitigation is unsuccessful, the VA may purchase the loan and take over servicing; however, this occurs rarely, and only if the circumstances causing delinquency were temporary and the veteran is able to resume payments.[152]

"HAMP-Style" Modifications: In 2009, the Obama Administration introduced the Home Affordable Modification Program (HAMP), an initiative to help borrowers who are behind on their mortgage payments.[153] Through HAMP, homeowners whose mortgage payments exceed 31% of their incomes (in general)[154], and who face additional hardships that make it difficult to remain current on their mortgages, may work with their loan servicers to modify their loans so that they are affordable. Technically, VA loans are not included as part of the HAMP program, but the VA has issued guidance requiring loan servicers to determine whether borrowers are eligible for "HAMP-style" modifications before proceeding with foreclosure or similar alternatives.[155] Where a borrower has missed payments and loss mitigation efforts have been unsuccessful, loan servicers are to evaluate the borrower to see if the loan could be modified through methods such as reduced interest rates or forebearance on principal payments to a point where the payments are at or below 31% of borrower income. If necessary, the VA will adjust its guaranty for larger loan amounts. Unlike HAMP (where loans must have originated on or before January 1, 2009), any VA-guaranteed loan is potentially eligible. If a lender and borrower enter into a modified loan, unlike HAMP, there is no trial period, and any reduced interest rate lasts for the life of the loan.

Mortgages That Are Underwater, But Current: In addition to increased foreclosures, the downturn in the economy has resulted in situations where some borrowers may have mortgages that exceed the value of their homes, sometimes referred to as being "underwater." This makes it difficult to refinance mortgages to take advantage of lower interest rates because lenders generally do not want to lend more than a home's appraised value. In cases where borrowers are current on their mortgage payments, but owe more than their homes are worth, they may qualify for an interest rate reduction refinancing loan (IRRRL) through the VA, despite the fact that their debt exceeds their homes' values.[156] Because an IRRRL does not require an appraisal, it is possible that some lenders may be willing to enter into a refinancing loan even where the loan exceeds the current property value.

Agreement between State Attorneys General and Large Mortgage Servicers: VA borrowers who are delinquent and/or underwater may also be eligible for assistance through an agreement reached between 49 state attorneys general,[157] the attorney general for the District of Columbia, and five large mortgage servicers in March 2012. Under the agreement, $25 billion is to be made available to assist certain borrowers.[158] In order to qualify for assistance, loans cannot have been purchased by Fannie Mae or Freddie Mac (and VA loans are not purchased by Fannie Mae or Freddie Mac), and they must be serviced by Bank of America, JPMorgan Chase, Wells Fargo, Citigroup, or Ally Financial. Pursuant to the settlement, the servicers must commit a minimum of $17 billion for foreclosure prevention, including principal reduction, and they must commit another $3 billion to assist underwater homeowners. Another $5 billion is to be awarded to the states, some of which, about $1.5 billion, will consist of payments to borrowers who lost their homes to foreclosure.[159]

Servicemembers Civil Relief Act: Another potential protection for borrowers may come through the Servicemembers Civil Relief Act (SCRA), which provides financial protections for active duty servicemembers, including home mortgage protections.[160] The act may assist veterans who entered into mortgages (including VA loans) prior to being called to active duty, and who are having trouble making their mortgage payments. In cases where a lender brings an action against a borrower for a mortgage obligation during a period of active duty, or within nine months after, the SCRA gives courts the authority to stay the proceedings.[161] In addition, the SCRA also generally declares invalid any foreclosure or home sale that takes place during this time period.

VA Actions in the Event of Foreclosure

If arrangements cannot be worked out to avoid foreclosure and properties proceed to sale, in most instances, loan servicers acquire the property at foreclosure sale and, in turn, sell it to the VA.[162] Whether a transfer to the VA occurs depends on the property value and the amount owed by the veteran borrower; each of these values is determined prior to the foreclosure sale.[163] The procedures that the VA goes through in order to determine when it will acquire a property, and for how much, were set up to ensure that the VA would not spend more than the amount for which the loan was guaranteed.[164] When a property goes to foreclosure, the VA will also pay the lender's claim against the guaranty. If the total indebtedness has been reduced over the life of the loan, then the guaranty is prorated,[165] and the guaranty is limited to the borrower's total indebtedness minus the VA's purchase price.[166]

Veterans who default on guaranteed loans are liable to the VA for losses suffered, and, in general, cannot have entitlement restored and obtain a new loan unless the loss is repaid to the VA.[167] The VA may waive the debt in cases where it determines collection "would be against equity and good conscience."[168] A veteran must request a waiver within one year of being notified about the debt. Circumstances that might result in a waiver could include job loss, disability, or other financial hardship. The VA may also accept a compromise payment and settle a debt for less than the amount owed.[169] **Table 9**, below, shows the number of properties with VA-guaranteed loans that are at some point in the foreclosure process, as well as foreclosed properties held in the VA inventory over the past decade. Since 2008, when the housing market began to experience difficulty, the number of homes with VA loans in foreclosure has increased. In 2011, the number of homes in foreclosure was double the highest previous number in the decade. Once the VA has acquired properties through the process of foreclosure, it attempts to resell them. In doing so, purchasers need not be veterans. In FY2011, the average time between VA acquisition of a foreclosed property and sale was seven months.[170] For more information about disposition of property, see the earlier section of this report entitled "Direct Loans Resulting from Borrower Delinquency or Default (Acquired and Vendee Loans)."

Table 9. VA Loans in Foreclosure Process and Foreclosed Properties in VA Inventory, FY2001-FY2011

Fiscal Year	Foreclosed Properties Held in VA Inventory[a]	Properties in the Foreclosure Process[b]
2001	14,543	8,425
2002	11,981	10,986
2003	11,832	10,513
2004	15,539	10,355
2005	7,288	6,597
2006	6,490	4,703
2007	6,975	4,696
2008	7,605	9,077
2009	8,464	17,000
2010	10,835	20,500
2011	7,322	22,000

Source: *VA Performance and Accountability Reports*, FY2002-FY2011. The reports are available on the VA website, http://www.va.gov/budget/report/index.asp.
a. Properties as of the end of the fiscal year.
b. The Performance and Accountability Reports do not indicate exactly what the "foreclosure process" entails.

End Notes

[1] 38 C.F.R. §36.4301.

[2] U.S. Congress, House Veterans' Affairs Committee, *The Historical Development of Veterans' Benefits in the United States, A Report on Veterans' Benefits in the United States*, committee print, prepared by The President's Commission on Veterans' Pensions, 84th Cong., 2nd sess., May 9, 1956, H.Prt. 84-244 (Washington: GPO, 1956), p. 161.

[3] Ibid.

[4] U.S. Congress, House Committee on World War Veterans' Legislation, *Providing Federal Government Aid for the Readjustment in Civilian Life of Returning World War II Veterans*, report to accompany S. 1767, 78th Cong., 2nd sess., May 5, 1944, H.Rept. 1418, p. 2.

[5] U.S. Congress, House Conference Committee, *Providing Federal Government Aid for the Readjustment to Civilian Life of Returning World War II Veterans*, report to accompany S. 1767, 78th Cong., 2nd sess., June 12, 1944, H.Rept.1624, pp. 162-163.

[6] 38 U.S.C. §101(2). For more information about who is a veteran, see CRS Report R42324, *"Who is a Veteran?"—Basic Eligibility for Veterans' Benefits*, by Christine Scott

[7] Reservists were made eligible as part of the Veterans Home Loan Program Amendments of 1992 (P.L. 102-547).

[8] 38 U.S.C. §3702(a)(2).

[9] See 38 U.S.C. §3710(g) and 38 C.F.R. §36.4340. Further guidance is at U.S. Department of Veterans Affairs, *Lenders Handbook – VA Pamphlet 26-7*, revised June 28, 2010, chapter 4, http://www.benefits.va.gov/warms/pam26_7.asp (hereinafter *VA Lenders Handbook*).

[10] 38 C.F.R. §36.4340(d).

[11] 38 C.F.R. §36.4340(f).

[12] *VA Lenders Handbook*, p. 4-55.

[13] 38 C.F.R. §36.4340(e).

[14] 38 C.F.R. §36.4340(g).

[15] Ibid.

[16] 38 U.S.C. §3710.

[17] 38 C.F.R. §36.4301.

[18] Ibid. There is an exception for a dwelling owned by more than one veteran—in that case there may be an extra unit for each additional veteran owner. For example, if three veterans owned a property together, it could consist of six units as long as three of the six units were occupied by the veteran owners.

[19] *VA Lenders Handbook*, p. 3-14.

[20] Ibid.

[21] 38 C.F.R. §36.4301.

[22] Ibid., definition of "residential property."

[23] 38 U.S.C. §3710(a)(9)(A)(ii).

[24] *VA Lenders Handbook*, Chapter 12.

[25] See VA response to questions for the record, U.S. Congress, House Committee on Veterans' Affairs, Subcommittee on Economic Opportunity, *Hearing on the Loan Guaranty Program*, 111th Cong., 2nd sess., May 20, 2010, p. 66.

[26] For a complete list of acceptable improvements, see 38 U.S.C. §3710(d).

[27] During the 1990s, the VA insured a decreasing number of manufactured housing units per year as reported in the VA Annual Reports. From FY1971 through FY1990, the VA guaranteed 112,786 manufactured home loans. U.S. Department of Veterans Affairs, *FY1990 Annual Report of the Secretary of Veterans Affairs*, March 1991, p. 29. In FY1991, the VA insured 313 loans, with this number decreasing to 126 in FY1992, 67 in FY1993, 24 in FY1994, 23 in FY1995, and 9 in FY1996, the last year in which manufactured home loans were separately noted in either the VA Annual Reports or the VA Annual Benefits Reports.

[28] This definition is from the manufactured housing portion of the regulations at 38 C.F.R. §36.4202. The definition of manufactured housing for the regular home loan guaranty at 38 C.F.R. §36.4301 is substantially the same.

[29] *VA Lenders Handbook*, p. 12-20.

[30] For state laws governing the titling of manufactured housing as well as the conversion of housing titled as a motor vehicle to real property, see the Fannie Mae website, https://www. efanniemae.com/sf/guides/ssg/relatedsellinginfo/manufachousing/titlingmanufhsing.jsp.

[31] U.S. Census Bureau, *Selected Characteristics of New Manufactured Homes Placed: By Region - 2010*, p. 1, http://www.census.gov/const/mhs/char10.pdf.

[32] U.S. Congress, Senate Labor and Public Welfare Committee, *Extension of Veterans' Home Loan Entitlements and Inclusion of Mobile Home Purchases*, report to accompany S. 3656, 91st Cong., 2nd sess., September 23, 1970, S.Rept. 91-1230, p. 13. When the Veterans' Housing Act (H.R. 16710) was considered and passed by the Senate, the bill was amended by and replaced with S. 3656, the companion bill to H.R. 16710, which contained a similar version of the loan guaranty program. See "Veterans' Housing Act of 1970," Senate debate, *Congressional Record*, vol. 116 (September 25, 1970), pp. 33781-33783.

[33] *Report of the President's Committee on the Vietnam Veteran*, Washington, DC, 1970, p. 33.

[34] Ibid.

[35] 38 U.S.C. §3712(d). The maximum loan terms are: single-wide, about 20 years for home and lot; double-wide, a maximum of 25 years for home and lot; or lot purchase, approximately 15 years.

[36] 38 U.S.C. §3710(a)(8) and (a)(9)(i).

[37] 38 U.S.C. §3710(a)(5).

[38] 38 U.S.C. §3710(e).

[39] Ibid.

[40] 38 U.S.C. §3710(e)(1)(C).

[41] U.S. Congress, House Committee on Veterans' Affairs, *Veterans' Housing Rehabilitation and Program Improvement Act of 1987*, report to accompany H.R. 2672, 100th Cong., 1st sess., July 30, 1987, H.Rept. 100-257, p. 15.

[42] *VA Lenders Handbook*, p. 6-2.

[43] Ibid., p. 3-3.

[44] Ibid., p. 10-10.

[45] Ibid., p. 6-18.

[46] U.S. Department of Housing and Urban Development and U.S. Department of Commerce, *American Housing Survey for the United States: 2009*, March 2011, p. 65, http://www. census.gov/prod/2011pubs/h150-09.pdf. See p. A-23 for the way in which "primary mortgage" status is determined.

[47] Statement of Tim S. Embree, Iraq and Afghanistan Veterans of America, U.S. Congress, House Committee on Veterans' Affairs, Subcommittee on Economic Opportunity, *Hearing on the Loan Guaranty Program*, 111th Cong., 2nd sess., May 20, 2010, pp. 51-52.

[48] For more information about Freddie Mac and the conforming loan limits, see CRS Report RS22172, *The Conforming Loan Limit*, by N. Eric Weiss and Sean M. Hoskins.

[49] P.L. 91-351, §305. The FHA statute was amended in 1969 to raise the limit to $33,000 (P.L. 91-152).

[50] P.L. 93-383, §805. The federal savings and loan limits on mortgage lending were codified at 12 U.S.C. §1464(c)(1976).

[51] P.L. 96-399, §313.

[52] Federal Housing Finance Agency, *History of Conforming Loan Limits*, http://www.fhfa.gov/ webfiles/860/loanlimitshistory07.pdf. Limits were increased in each year with the exception of 1990.

[53] P.L. 111-5 returned the limit for high-cost areas to the level first instituted in 2008 as part of the Economic Stimulus Act of 2008 (P.L. 110-185).

[54] 38 U.S.C. §3703.

[55] 38 U.S.C. §3703(a)(1)(C).

[56] 12 U.S.C. §1454.

[57] This is based on the provision in the Freddie Mac statute for areas where 115% of median home prices exceed the conforming loan limit. 12 U.S.C. §1454(a)(2)(C). See the text box for more information.

[58] For FY2012 county limits see http://www.benefits.va.gov/HOMELOANS/docs/Loan_Limits_2012_Dec_2011.pdf.

[59] U.S. Department of Veterans Affairs, *FY2011 Annual Benefits Report*, p. 66, http://www.vba.va.gov/REPORTS/abr/2011_abr.pdf.

[60] 12 U.S.C. §1454(a)(2)(C).

[61] The higher conforming loan limit for Alaska, Hawaii, and Guam was introduced in 1980 (P.L. 96-399). The U.S. Virgin Islands was added to the list in 1992 (P.L. 102-550). See also, U.S. Congress, Conference Report, report to accompany S. 2719, 96th Cong., 2nd sess., *September* 26, 1980, H.Rept. 96-1420, p. 117.

[62] See http://www.benefits.va.gov/HOMELOANS/docs/Loan_Limits_2012_Dec_2011.pdf.

[63] U.S. Department of Veterans Affairs, *VA Circular 26-08-19, Implementation of Loan Guaranty Provisions of P.L. 110-389* , October 16, 2008, p. 2, http://www.benefits.va.gov/homeloans/docs/26_08_19.pdf.

[64] Based on this, the greatest amount of guaranty for which a veteran could qualify in a high-cost area was $273,656.25 (($625,500 * 1.75) * .25).

[65] See, for example, the 2011 VA County Loan Limits for High-Cost Counties, http://www.benefits.va.gov/homeloans/docs/2011_county_loan_limits.pdf.

[66] *The Ginnie Mae Mortgage Backed Securities Guide*, August 1, 2011, p. 9-1, http://www.ginniemae.gov/guide/pdf/ chap09.pdf.

[67] *VA Lenders Handbook*, p. 3-9.

[68] 38 U.S.C. §3703(a).

[69] *VA Lenders Handbook*, pp. 3-12 and 3-14.

[70] 38 U.S.C. §3702(b).

[71] Ibid. See also *VA Lenders Handbook*, p. 2-15.

[72] *VA Lenders Handbook*, p. 2-15.

[73] Ibid., p. 3-9.

[74] See CRS Report RS20530, *FHA-Insured Home Loans: An Overview*, by Katie Jones.

[75] Ibid.

[76] Ibid.

[77] 38 C.F.R. §36.4313.

[78] See *VA Lenders Handbook*, p. 8-7.

[79] U.S. Department of Housing and Urban Development, *Handbook 4155.2, Lender's Guide to the Single Family Mortgage Insurance Process*, p. 6-A-12, http://portal.hud.gov/hudportal/documents/huddoc?id=4155-2_6_secA.pdf.

[80] CRS Report RS20530, *FHA-Insured Home Loans: An Overview*, by Katie Jones.

[81] 38 U.S.C. §3731 requires the VA Secretary to set up a process for approving appraisers that includes a testing process and recommendations from other appraisers, and to develop and maintain a list of approved appraisers.

[82] *VA Lenders Handbook*, chapter 15.

[83] See Section 2(1)(B)(ii)(I). Just prior to the enactment of P.L. 107-326, veteran borrowers qualified for a principle balance of 100% of the first $25,000 of the appraised value, compared to 97% for non-veteran borrowers. In addition, the maximum principle balance on amounts above $125,000 was 90% for non-veteran borrowers, compared to 95% for veteran borrowers.

[84] See Section 2113 of P.L. 110-289.

[85] U.S. Congress, Senate Committee on Banking and Currency, *Housing Act of 1950*, report to accompany S. 2246, 81st Cong., 2nd sess., February 24, 1950, S.Rept. 81-1286, p. 92.

[86] The old U.S. Code Section, 38 U.S.C. §694*l* (1952), was replaced by 38 U.S.C. §1811 (1958). See the table of contents for Title 38 of the U.S. Code 1958 version.

[87] U.S. Congress, House Committee on Veterans' Affairs, Subcommittee on Housing, *Bills to Provide for Purchase of Mobile Homes Under Veterans' Administration Guaranty and Other Bills Related to Veterans' Housing*, 91st Cong., 2nd sess., July 14 and 16, 1970, pp. 3461-3462.

[88] 38 U.S.C. §3711.

[89] U.S. Veterans Administration, *Annual Report 1981*, May 1982, p. 71.

[90] For example, the language in the FY2012 Consolidated Appropriations Act (P.L. 112-74) was "not to exceed$500,000 in gross obligations for direct loans are authorized for specially adapted housing loans." According to the Conference Committee Report, the law "limits obligations for direct loans to not more than $500,000." See H.Rept. 111-366.

[91] U.S. Department of Veterans Affairs, *FY2013 Congressional Budget Submission, Volume III, Benefits and Burial Programs and Departmental Administration*, pp. 2E-1 and 2E-6, http://www.va.gov/budget/docs/summary/Fy2013_Volume_III-Benefits_Burial_Dept_Admin.pdf (hereinafter FY2013 VA Budget Justifications).

[92] See U.S. Department of Veterans Affairs, *M26-1 Guaranteed Loan Processing Manual*, p. 10-15, http://www.benefits.va.gov/warms/M26_1.asp.

[93] 38 U.S.C. §3765(3). The statute refers to "Pacific Islander" as one who is "who is indigenous to a United States territory or possession located in the Pacific Ocean," as defined by the Native American Programs Act of 1974, 42 U.S.C. §2992c(7). The three U.S. territories in the Pacific are American Samoa, Guam, and the Commonwealth of the Northern Mariana Islands.

[94] U.S. Congress, Senate Committee on Veterans' Affairs, *Veterans Benefits and Health Care Act of 1989*, report to accompany S. 13, 101st Cong., 1st sess., September 13, 1989, S.Rept. 101-126 (Washington: GPO, 1989), pp. 290-291. The Senate amended H.R. 901 (which would ultimately become P.L. 101-237) with provisions from S. 13.

[95] U.S. Department of the Interior, *DOI Trust Reform: As-Is Trust Business Model Report*, March 21, 2003, p. 2-1, http://www.ost.doi.gov/trust_reform/roadmap.html.

[96] U.S. Department of Agriculture, *Lending on Native American Lands: A Guide for Rural Development Staff*, June2006, p. 24, http://www.rurdev.usda.gov/rd/aian/LendingOnNative Lands_RD.pdf.

[97] See U.S. Congress, Senate Committee on Veterans' Affairs, *Native American Veterans Home Loan Equity Act of1992*, report to accompany S. 2528, 102nd Cong., August 12, 1992, S.Rept. 102-378, p. 11. Quoting from an evaluation of VA lending on tribal land, the report stated that "The inability to use tribal land as security for a mortgage loan is the most significant factor in limiting access to the VA loan guaranty benefit that can be affected by VA." S. 2528 was incorporated into P.L. 102-547. See "Veterans Home Loan Program Revitalization Act of 1992," House debate, *Congressional Record*, vol. 138, part 22 (October 5, 1992), p. 32374.

[98] See the Department of the Interior website, "Insular Area Summary for American Samoa," http://www.doi.gov/oia/Islandpages/asgpage.htm.

[99] AM. SAMOA CODE ANN. §37.0204.

[100] N.M.I. Const., Art. XII, Sec. 1.

[101] Congress, in response to the concerns of the Advisory Committee on Native American Veterans, directed the Departments of Veterans Affairs and Interior to look into the extent to which Native American veterans on trust land participated in the loan guaranty program and release a report (see the Veterans' Benefits Amendments of 1989 (P.L. 101-237)). The findings of the report are summarized in S.Rept. 102-378, p. 10.

[102] The MOU is available at http://www.benefits.va.gov/homeloans/docs/mou.pdf.

[103] U.S. Department of Veterans Affairs, Annual Benefits Report FY2011, p. 63, http://www.vba.va.gov/REPORTS/abr/2011_abr.pdf.

[104] Ibid.

[105] U.S. Congress, Senate Committee on Veterans' Affairs, Pending Benefits-Related Legislation, 109th Cong., 1st sess., June 23, 2005, S.Hrg. 109-243, p. 27.

[106] Ibid., p. 28.

[107] E-mail communication from the VA, April 13, 2012.

[108] U.S. Department of Veterans Affairs, *FY2011 Performance and Accountability Report*, November 15, 2011, p. III-13, http://www.va.gov/budget/docs/report/2011-VAPAR_FullWeb.pdf (hereinafter *FY2011 Performance and Accountability Report*).

[109] 38 U.S.C. §§3733(a)(1) and (a)(7).

[110] See *FY2011 Performance and Accountability Report*, pp. III-30 to III-31. Congress authorized the VA to guarantee principal and interest payments on these certificates as part of P.L. 102-291, which is codified at 38 U.S.C. §3720(h).

[111] *FY2011 Performance and Accountability Report*, p. III-31.

[112] FY2013 VA Budget Justifications, p. 2E-4.

[113] E-mail communication from the VA, April 13, 2012.

[114] The FCRA was part of the Omnibus Reconciliation Act of 1990. It is found under Title XIII, Budget Enforcement, as Title V, Credit Reform.

[115] Ibid.

[116] The reestimates are part of the Supplemental Materials on the OMB Budget website. There are tables for reestimates of direct loan subsidy rates and loan guarantee subsidy rates. See Office of Management and Budget, *FY2013 Federal Credit Supplement*, pp. 73-74 for guaranteed loans and pp. 49-50 for direct loans, http://www.whitehouse.gov/sites/default/files/omb/budget/fy2013/assets/cr_supp.pdf.

[117] 38 U.S.C. §3722. The fund was instituted in 1998 as part of P.L. 105-368, the Veterans Programs Enhancement Act. Prior to this, the loan guaranty and direct loan programs had been funded through three accounts, the Guaranty and Indemnity Fund, and two liquidating accounts.

[118] 38 U.S.C. §3729.

[119] 38 U.S.C. §3729(c).

[120] 38 U.S.C. §3729(a). See also, *VA Lenders Handbook*, p. 3-11.

[121] The Veterans' Readjustment Benefits Act of 1966 (P.L. 89-358) imposed a fee of 0.5% on veterans who served during the post-Korean War era, but this fee was withdrawn four years later as part of the Veterans' Housing Act of 1970 (P.L. 91-506).

[122] The letter and draft legislation were made part of the House Veterans' Affairs Committee report for H.R. 6782, a bill where the section regarding loan fees was eventually incorporated into the Omnibus Budget Reconciliation Act of 1982 (P.L. 97-253). See CQ Almanac 1982, 38th ed., *Reconciliation Savings: $130 Billion by 1985*, 1983, pp. 199-204, http://library.cqpress.com/cqalmanac/cqal82-1164004. The VA administrator letter is at U.S. Congress, House Committee on Veterans' Affairs, *Veterans' Disability Compensation and Survivors' Benefits Amendments of 1982*, report to accompany H.R. 6782, 97th Cong., 2nd sess., July 23, 1982, H.Rept. 97-660, pp. 49-50.

[123] Ibid.

[124] See, for example, U.S. Congress, House Committee on Veterans' Affairs, Subcommittee on Housing and Memorial Affairs, *VA Home Loan Guaranty Program*, 97th Cong., 2nd sess., March 23, 1982.

[125] Note that prior to the extension of existing fees in P.L. 108-183, in August 2011 the Restoring GI Bill Fairness Act of 2011 (P.L. 112-26) changed fees for subsequent loans with less than 5% down payment for both active duty veterans and reservists.

[126] See U.S. Department of Veterans Affairs, *VA Circular 26-11-15, Updated Funding Fee Changes*, October 6, 2011, http://www.benefits.va.gov/HOMELOANS/circulars/26_11_15.pdf and *VA Circular 26-11-19, Funding Fee Update as of November 22, 2011*, November 22, 2011, http://www.benefits.va.gov/homeloans/circulars/26_11_19.pdf.

[127] The Specially Adapted Housing Program is codified at 38 U.S.C. §§2101-2107.

[128] The first is addressed in 38 U.S.C. §2101(a) and the second in 38 U.S.C. §2101(b).

[129] 38 C.F.R. §3.809.

[130] See U.S. Congress, Senate Committee on Veterans' Affairs, *Veterans' Disability Compensation and Housing Benefits Amendments of 1980*, report to accompany S. 2649, 96th Cong., 2nd sess., July 30, 1980, S.Rept. 96-876, pp. 24-26.

[131] The resulting report was published as a committee print, U.S. Congress, House Committee on Veterans' Affairs, *The Needs of Veterans Who Are Totally Blind from Service-Connected Causes for Home Modifications*, committee print, prepared by Veterans' Administration, 96th Cong., 2nd sess., January 11, 1980, H.Prt. 96-56.

[132] U.S. Congress, Senate Committee on Veterans' Affairs, *Veterans' Disability Compensation and Housing Benefits Amendments of 1980*, report to accompany S. 2649, 96th Cong., 2nd sess., July 30, 1980, S.Rept. 96-876, pp. 25-26.

[133] 38 C.F.R. §3.809a.

[134] U.S. Congress, House Committee on Veterans' Affairs, *Veterans Housing and Employment Improvement Act of 2005*, report to accompany H.R. 3665, 109th Cong., 1st sess., November 1, 2005, H.Rept. 109-263, p. 13.

[135] The cost of construction index is to reflect the average change in construction costs from year to year. The VA chose an existing index, the Turner Building Cost Index. See U.S. Department of Veterans Affairs, "Loan Guaranty: Assistance to Eligible Individuals in Acquiring Specially Adapted Housing; Cost-of-Construction Index," 74 *Federal Register* 48658, September 24, 2009.

[136] See VA website, "VA Announces Amounts of Assistance for Veterans Under the VA Specially Adapted Housing Program for Fiscal Year 2012," http://www.benefits.va.gov/HOMELOANS/docs/website_alert_2012.pdf.

[137] U.S. Department of Veterans Affairs, *FY2009 Performance and Accountability Report*, November 16, 2009, p. II-4, http://www.va.gov/budget/report/index.asp.

[138] 38 C.F.R. §36.4405.

[139] U.S. Department of Veterans Affairs, "Loan Guaranty: Assistance to Eligible Individuals in Obtaining Specially Adapted Housing ," 75 *Federal Register* 56875-56880, September 17, 2010. In advance of the final rule, the VA had issued guidance broadening property ownership categories. See U.S. Department of Veterans Affairs, *Circular 26-08-5, Expansion of the Types of Ownership Interests Permissible Under the Specially Adapted Housing (SAH) Grant Program*, March 10, 2008, http://www.benefits.va.gov/homeloans/circulars/26_08_5.pdf.

[140] 38 C.F.R. §36.4401.

[141] National Bureau of Economic Research, *Determination of the December 2007 Peak in Economic Activity*, December 11, 2008, http://www.nber.org/cycles/dec2008.pdf.

[142] Mortgage Bankers Association, *National Delinquency Survey, First Quarter 2007*, data as of March 31, 2007, p. 3, and *National Delinquency Survey, Fourth Quarter 2011*, data as of December 31, 2011, p. 3.

[143] The Mortgage Bankers Association releases quarterly National Delinquency Surveys with delinquency and foreclosure data that includes subprime loans, prime loans, FHA loans, and VA loans. From 2002 to the present, the VA foreclosure rate has been lower than the FHA foreclosure rate; since 2007, the VA foreclosure rate has been lower than the rate for all loans; and since the end of 2010, the VA loan foreclosure rate has been lower than fixed-rate prime loans.

[144] Mortgage Bankers Association, National Delinquency Surveys, see footnote 142.

[145] See, for example, Historical Statistics of the United States, *Table Dc1255-1270, Mortgage foreclosures and delinquencies: 1926-1979*, http://hsus.cambridge.org/HSUSWeb/toc/table Toc.do?id=Dc1255-1270, and Mortgage Bankers Association Historical National Delinquency Survey Data.

[146] Statement of Thomas J. Pamperin, VA Associate Deputy Under Secretary for Policy and Program Management, U.S. Congress, House Committee on Veterans' Affairs,

Subcommittee on Economic Opportunity, *Hearing on the Loan Guaranty Program*, 111th Cong., 2nd sess., May 20, 2010, pp. 22-23.

[147] 38 C.F.R. §36.4319.

[148] U.S. Department of Veterans Affairs, "Loan Guaranty: Loan Servicing and Claims Procedures Modifications," 73*Federal Register* 6294-6368, February 1, 2008.

[149] 38 C.F.R. §36.4315.

[150] U.S. Department of Veterans Affairs, "Loan Guaranty Revised Loan Modification Procedures," 76 *Federal Register* 6555-6559, February 7, 2011.

[151] U.S. Department of Veterans Affairs, *VA Loan Electronic Reporting Interface VA Servicer Guide*, July 31, 2009, p.87, http://www.benefits.va.gov/homeloans/docs/va_servicer_guide.pdf.

[152] 38 C.F.R. §36.4320.

[153] For more information about HAMP and other foreclosure prevention initiatives, see CRS Report R40210, *Preserving Homeownership: Foreclosure Prevention Initiatives*, by Katie Jones.

[154] Until June 1, 2012, in order to participate in HAMP, borrowers were required to have mortgage payments that exceeded 31% of their income. However, the Obama Administration announced "HAMP Tier II" on March 9, 2012, in order to try to assist additional borrowers. Beginning June 1, 2012, borrowers may have mortgage payments that makeup less than 31% of their income and still qualify for HAMP. See *Making Home Affordable Supplemental Directive 12-02*, March 9, 2012, https://www.hmpadmin.com/portal/programs/docs/hamp_servicer/sd1202.pdf.

[155] U.S. Department of Veterans Affairs, *Circular 26-10-6, Revised VA Making Home Affordable Program*, May 24, 2010, http://www.benefits.va.gov/homeloans/circulars/26_10_6.pdf.

[156] VA Circular 26-10-6 states that veterans who are current on their VA-guaranteed loans should be evaluated for the IRRRL.

[157] Oklahoma was not a party to the agreement.

[158] U.S. Department of Justice, "Federal Government and State Attorneys General Reach $25 Billion Agreement with Five Largest Mortgage Servicers to Address Mortgage Loan Servicing and Foreclosure Abuses," press release, February 9, 2012, http://www.justice.gov/opa/pr/2012/February/12-ag-186.html.

[159] For more information, see the website devoted to the settlement, http://www.nationalmortgagesettlement.com/.

[160] For more information, see CRS Report RL34575, *The Servicemembers Civil Relief Act (SCRA): An Explanation*, by R. Chuck Mason.

[161] 50 U.S.C. Appendix §533.

[162] Veterans Benefits Administration Powerpoint Presentation, "Loan Guaranty Program Overview."

[163] 38 U.S.C. §3732(c) gives the VA the authority to purchase property from the loan servicer where the net value of the property exceeds the unguaranteed portion of the loan. Further, pursuant to 38 C.F.R. §36.4323(b), the VA may acquire properties even where the net value does not exceed the unguaranteed portion of the debt. However, in these cases, the servicer must waive the amount of the indebtedness that exceeds the net value (i.e., the servicer will not pursue the veteran borrower for the deficiency) for the VA to be able to accept the transfer.

[164] See U.S. Congress, conference report to accompany H.R. 4170, 98th Cong., 2nd sess., June 23, 1984, H.Rept. 98-861, pp. 1374-1375.

[165] See 38 U.S.C. §3703(b): "The liability of the United States under any guaranty, within the limitations of this chapter, shall decrease or increase pro rata with any decrease or increase of the amount of the unpaid portion of the obligation." But "[i]n no event may the liability of the United States under a guaranteed loan exceed the amount guaranteed with respect to that loan under section 3703 (b) of this title." 38 U.S.C. §3732(c)(9).

[166] 38 U.S.C. §3732(c)(5). The VA pays the "net value" for the property—its fair market value minus costs the VA would incur while holding the property.

[167] 38 U.S.C. §3702(b).

[168] 38 U.S.C. §5302(b).

[169] 38 U.S.C. §3720(a).

[170] *FY2011 Performance and Accountability Report*, November 15, 2011, p. III-33.

In: Veteran Housing Assistance   ISBN: 978-1-62417-369-1
Editor: Craig Del Monte   © 2013 Nova Science Publishers, Inc.

Chapter 2

VETERANS AND HOMELESSNESS*

Libby Perl

SUMMARY

The wars in Iraq and Afghanistan have brought renewed attention to the needs of veterans, including the needs of homeless veterans. Both male and female veterans have been overrepresented in the homeless population, and as the number of veterans increases due to these conflicts, there is concern that the number of homeless veterans could rise commensurately. The recent economic downturn also has raised concerns that homelessness could increase among all groups, including veterans.

Congress has created numerous programs that serve homeless veterans specifically, almost all of which are funded through the Veterans Health Administration. These programs provide health care and rehabilitation services for homeless veterans (the Health Care for Homeless Veterans and Domiciliary Care for Homeless Veterans programs), employment assistance (Homeless Veterans Reintegration Program and Compensated Work Therapy program), and transitional housing (Grant and Per Diem program) as well as other supportive services. The VA also works with the Department of Housing and Urban Development (HUD) to provide permanent supportive housing to homeless veterans through the HUD-VA Supported Housing Program (HUD-

---

* This is an edited, reformatted and augmented version of the Congressional Research Service Publication, CRS Report for Congress RL34024, dated February 2, 2012.

VASH). In the HUD-VASH program, HUD funds rental assistance through Section 8 vouchers while the VA provides supportive services. In addition, two newly enacted programs focus on homelessness prevention through supportive services: the VA's Supportive Services for Veteran Families program and a VA and HUD homelessness prevention demonstration program.

Several issues regarding veterans and homelessness have become prominent, in part because of the Iraq and Afghanistan wars. One issue is ending homelessness among veterans. In November 2009, the VA announced a plan to end homelessness within five years. Both the VA and HUD have taken steps to increase housing and services for homeless veterans. Funding for VA programs has increased in recent years (see **Table 6**) and Congress has appropriated funds to increase available units of permanent supportive housing through the HUD-VASH program (see **Table 7**). In each of the FY2008, FY2009, and FY2010 HUD appropriations acts, Congress provided funds sufficient to support more than 10,000 new Section 8 vouchers per year, which have been distributed to housing authorities in all 50 states, the District of Columbia, Puerto Rico, and Guam. The FY2011 Department of Defense and Full-Year Continuing Appropriations Act (P.L. 112-10) provided an additional $50 million for HUD-VASH (funding 6,790 vouchers), and the FY2012 Consolidated and Further Continuing Appropriations Act (P.L. 112-55) brought the funding level back to $75 million. Estimates of the number of veterans experiencing homelessness have grown smaller, perhaps due in part to the infusion of vouchers for permanent supportive housing.

Another issue is the concern that veterans returning from Iraq and Afghanistan who are at risk of homelessness may not receive the services they need. In addition, concerns have risen about the needs of female veterans, whose numbers are increasing. Women veterans face challenges that could contribute to their risks of homelessness. They are more likely to have experienced sexual trauma than women in the general population and are more likely than male veterans to be single parents. Few homeless programs for veterans have the facilities to provide separate accommodations for women and women with children.

INTRODUCTION

The wars in Iraq and Afghanistan have brought renewed attention to the needs of veterans, including the needs of homeless veterans. Homeless veterans initially came to the country's attention in the 1970s and 1980s, when homelessness generally was becoming a more prevalent and noticeable phenomenon. The first section of this report defines the term "homeless veteran," discusses attempts to estimate the number of veterans who are homeless, and presents the results of studies regarding the demographic characteristics of homeless veterans as well as those served in VA homeless programs. At the same time that the number of homeless persons began to grow, it became clear through various analyses of homeless individuals that homeless veterans were overrepresented in the homeless population. The second section of this report summarizes the available research regarding the overrepresentation of both male and female veterans, who have been found to be present in greater percentages in the homeless population than their percentages in the general population. This section also reviews research regarding possible explanations for why homeless veterans have been overrepresented. In response to the issue of homelessness among veterans, the federal government has created numerous programs to fund services and transitional housing specifically for homeless veterans. The third section of this report discusses these programs. The majority of programs are funded through the Department of Veterans Affairs (VA). Within the VA, the Veterans Health Administration (VHA), which is responsible for the health care of veterans, operates all but one of the programs for homeless veterans. The Veterans Benefits Administration (VBA), which is responsible for compensation, pensions, educational assistance, home loan guarantees, and insurance, operates the other. In addition, the Department of Labor (DOL) and the Department of Housing and Urban Development (HUD) operate programs for homeless veterans. Several issues regarding homelessness among veterans have become prominent since the beginning of the conflicts in Iraq and Afghanistan. The fourth section of this report discusses three of these issues. The first is the VA's plan to end homelessness among veterans. A second issue is ensuring that an adequate transition process exists for returning veterans to assist them with issues that might put them at risk of homelessness. Third is the concern that adequate services might not exist to serve the needs of women veterans.

OVERVIEW OF VETERANS AND HOMELESSNESS

Homelessness has always existed in the United States, but only in recent decades has the issue come to prominence. In the 1970s and 1980s, the number of homeless persons increased, as did their visibility. Experts cite various causes for the increase in homelessness. These include the demolition of single room occupancy dwellings in so-called "skid rows" where transient single men lived, the decreased availability of affordable housing generally, the reduced need for seasonal unskilled labor, the reduced likelihood that relatives will accommodate homeless family members, the decreased value of public benefits, and changed admissions standards at mental hospitals.[1] The increased visibility of homeless persons was due, in part, to the decriminalization of actions such as public drunkenness, loitering, and vagrancy.[2]

Homelessness occurs among families with children and single individuals, in rural communities as well as large urban cities, and for varying periods of time. Depending on circumstances, periods of homelessness may vary from days to years. Researchers have created three categories of homelessness based on the amount of time that individuals are homeless.[3] First, transitionally homeless people are those who have one short stay in a homeless shelter before returning to permanent housing. In the second category, those who are episodically homeless frequently move in and out of homelessness but do not remain homeless for long periods of time. Third, chronically homeless individuals are those who are homeless continuously for a period of one year or have at least four episodes of homelessness in three years. Chronically homeless individuals often suffer from mental illness and/or substance use disorders. Although veterans experience all types of homelessness, they are thought to be chronically homeless in higher numbers than nonveterans.[4]

Homeless veterans began to come to the attention of the public at the same time that homelessness generally was becoming more common. News accounts chronicled the plight of veterans who had served their country but were living (and dying) on the street.[5] The commonly held notion that the military experience provides young people with job training, educational and other benefits, as well as the maturity needed for a productive life, conflicted with the presence of veterans among the homeless population.[6]

Definition of "Homeless Veteran"

In order to qualify for assistance under the homeless veteran programs governed by Title 38 of the U.S. Code, veterans must meet the definition of "homeless veteran." Although the term "homeless veteran" might appear straightforward, it contains two layers of definition.[7] First, the definition of "veteran" for purposes of Title 38 benefits (the Title of the United States Code that governs veterans benefits) is a person who "served in the active military, naval, or air service" and was not dishonorably discharged.[8] For a detailed discussion of the criteria required to receive veterans benefits, see *"Who is a Veteran?"—Basic Eligibility for Veterans' Benefits*, by Christine Scott.

Second, veterans are considered homeless if they meet the definition of "homeless individual" codified as part of the McKinney-Vento Homeless Assistance Act (P.L. 100-77).[9] Specifically, the statute defining homeless veteran refers to Section 103(a) of McKinney-Vento. Until recently, Section 103(a) defined a homeless individual as (1) an individual who lacks a fixed, regular, and adequate nighttime residence, and (2) a person who has a nighttime residence that is

- a supervised publicly or privately operated shelter designed to provide temporary living accommodations (including welfare hotels, congregate shelters, and transitional housing for the mentally ill);
- an institution that provides a temporary residence for individuals intended to be institutionalized; or
- a public or private place not designed for, nor ordinarily used as, a regular sleeping accommodation for human beings.

However, legislation was enacted in the 111th Congress that expanded the definition of "homeless individual" under McKinney-Vento: The Homeless Emergency Assistance and Rapid Transition to Housing (HEARTH) Act (P.L. 111-22). HUD issued regulations regarding the new definition of homelessness in December 2011, and they took effect on January 4, 2012. The HEARTH Act added categories to the way in which a person may experience homelessness, and moved away from what had been a requirement for literal homelessness.[10] These changes also affect the way in which "homeless veteran" is defined.

- **Imminent Loss of Housing:** P.L. 111-22 added to the current definition those individuals and families who meet all of the following criteria: (1) They will "imminently lose their housing," whether it be their own housing, housing they are sharing with others, or a hotel or motel not paid for by a government entity. Imminent loss of housing is evidenced by an eviction notice requiring an individual or family to leave their housing within 14 days; a lack of resources that would allow an individual or family to remain in a hotel or motel for more than 14 days; or credible evidence that an individual or family would not be able to stay with another homeowner or renter for more than 14 days. (2) They have no subsequent residence identified. (3) They lack the resources needed to obtain other permanent housing. (HUD practice prior to passage of the HEARTH Act was to consider those individuals and families who would imminently lose housing within seven days to be homeless.)

- **Other Federal Definitions:** In addition, P.L. 111-22 added to the definition of "homeless individual" unaccompanied youth and homeless families with children who are defined as homeless under other federal statutes and who (1) have experienced a long-term period without living independently in permanent housing; (2) have experienced instability as evidenced by frequent moves; and (3) can be expected to continue in unstable housing due to factors such as chronic disabilities, chronic physical health or mental health conditions, substance addiction, histories of domestic violence or childhood abuse, the presence of a child or youth with a disability, or multiple barriers to employment.

Another change to the definition of homeless individual is to consider anyone who is fleeing a situation of domestic violence or some other life-threatening condition to be homeless. However, this provision was added to Section 103(b) of McKinney-Vento, so unless the reference to "homeless veteran" in Title 38 is changed to include subsection (b), this part of the definition is not explicitly part of the definition of homeless veteran.

Estimates of the Number of Homeless Veterans

The exact number of homeless veterans is unknown, although the methods used to estimate their numbers have been improving in recent years. Until 2011, both the VA and HUD conducted separate assessments of the number and percentage of homeless veterans over a period of years (the VA beginning in 1998, and HUD in 2006). However, beginning in 2011, the two agencies announced that they would coordinate their efforts and use one count as "the definitive estimate of veteran homelessness."[11] This estimate comes from the HUD biennial "point-in-time" count of homeless individuals. The point-in-time counts began in 2005, with HUD requiring local jurisdictions called "Continuums of Care" (CoCs)[12] to conduct a count of sheltered and unsheltered homeless persons on one night during the last week of January every other year (though many CoCs conduct counts every year). As part of these point-in-time counts, CoCs are to collect information about homeless individuals, including veteran status.

In order to understand what the estimates of homeless veterans represent, it is important to understand how the HUD process for estimating the number of homeless people works. Since 2005, HUD has issued six Annual Homeless Assessment Reports (AHARs) to Congress. In addition to point-in-time estimates, the AHARS include year-long estimates of the number of people experiencing homelessness. AHAR estimates have included the number of homeless veterans since 2009. The estimates operate as follows:

- **Point-in-Time Estimate:** The point-in-time counts are a snapshot of the number of people who are homeless on a given day, and they are not meant to represent the total number of people who experience homelessness over the course of a year.[13] Until 2011, communities were not required to count unsheltered individuals—those living on the street or in other places not meant for human habitation—although most communities did (approximately 84% conducted both a sheltered and unsheltered count).[14] Beginning in 2011, all communities are required to count those living on the streets or other places not meant for human habitation.[15]

- **Year-Long Estimate:** The second HUD estimate is an ongoing process to produce an *annual* estimate of the number of people who are homeless, including homeless veterans, through Homeless Management Information Systems (HMIS) through which local jurisdictions collect and store information about homeless individuals they serve, and the information is aggregated in computer systems at the community level. The estimates based on HMIS data differ from point-in-time estimates in that they are based on a full year's worth of information (rather than one day) and based on a sample of communities (rather than an aggregation of all communities). These estimates only include those persons who were residing in emergency shelters or transitional housing during the relevant time periods (i.e., estimates do not include those persons living on the street or in similar places not meant for human habitation).

In the two most recent AHARs (2009 and 2010), HUD and the VA together have released a Veterans Supplement to the AHAR. Prior to 2009, HUD had released four AHARs that included overall estimates of the number of homeless individuals, but only the *percentage* of veterans who were homeless, not the number. However, the 2009 and 2010 veterans supplements provided estimates and descriptive information about veterans experiencing homelessness. In addition, HUD released the 2011 point-in-time results on December 13, 2011, which include an estimate of homeless veterans.

This section of the report discusses the estimates included in the veterans supplements to HUD's Annual Homeless Assessment Reports for 2009 and 2010, the 2011 point-in-time count results, as well as the VA's previous efforts to estimate the number of homeless veterans. See **Table 1** for the estimates for the last three years.

2009 Homeless Veterans Supplement to the AHAR

The fifth AHAR included a separate analysis of both point-in-time and HMIS data regarding the number of veterans experiencing homelessness.[16] As with the point-in-time count for the AHAR generally, the veterans supplement included an estimate of the number of sheltered and unsheltered veterans experiencing homelessness on one night in January 2009. The estimate derived from HMIS data was an estimate of the number of veterans living in shelter who were homeless at any point from October 1, 2008, through September 30, 2009.

- **Point-in-Time Estimate:** The veterans supplement estimated that 75,609 veterans experienced homelessness on one night in January 2009.[17] The estimate relied on local CoC point-in-time reports, but researchers adjusted the data to account for missing data, specifically (1) cases where beds for homeless veterans were missing from HUD's inventory of service providers, (2) instances where data on sheltered veteran status were missing, (3) instances where CoCs did not count sheltered veterans, and (4) instances of missing data on unsheltered veterans or reports of zero unsheltered veterans.[18] Of the 75,609 homeless veterans, a reported 57% were sleeping in emergency shelter or transitional housing and 43% were on the street or in other places not meant for human habitation.[19]
- **HMIS Estimate:** Using data from a sample of 300 communities, researchers estimated that 136,334 veterans were homeless on at least one night from October 1, 2008, through September 30, 2009.[20] The data reported by local CoCs were adjusted to account for sheltered adults whose veteran status was unknown and for emergency shelters

and transitional housing facilities that did not report data to the local HMIS.[21]

Table 1. HUD Annual Homeless Assessment Reports: Estimates of Homeless Veterans, 2009-2011

Type of Estimate	Population Included in Estimate	2009			2010			2011		
		# of Homeless Veterans	% of Adult Homeless Population		# of Homeless Veterans	% of Adult Homeless Population		# of Homeless Veterans	% of Adult Homeless Population	
Point-in-time	Veterans living in shelter, on the street, or other places not meant for human habitation.	75,609	16%		76,329	16%		67,495	14%	
Year-long	Veterans living in shelter.	136,334	10%		144,842	13%		—[a]	—[a]	

Source: U.S. Department of Housing and Urban Development and U.S. Department of Veterans Affairs, *Veteran Homelessness: A Supplemental Report to the 2009 Annual Homeless Assessment Report to Congress*, January 2011, http://www.hudhre.info/documents/2009AHARVeteransReport.pdf; U.S. Department of Housing and Urban Development and U.S. Department of Veterans Affairs, *Veteran Homelessness: A Supplemental Report to the 2010 Annual Homeless Assessment Report to Congress*, October 2011, http://www.hudhre.info/documents/2010AHARVeteransReports.pdf; and U.S. Department of Housing and Urban Development, *The 2011 Point-in-Time Estimates of Homelessness: Supplement to the Annual Homeless Assessment Report*, December 2011, p. 6, http://www.hudhre.info/documents/PIT-HIC_SupplementalAHARReport.pdf.

a. The 2011 AHAR with its year-long estimate of homeless veterans has not yet been released.

In both the point-in-time estimate and the HMIS estimate, veterans were overrepresented in the homeless population. According to the point-in-time estimate, veterans represented 16% of the adult homeless population (compared to 8% of the total population), and in the HMIS estimate veterans were about 10% of the homeless population.[22]

2010 Homeless Veterans Supplement to the AHAR

The veterans supplement to the sixth AHAR included an estimate of the number of sheltered and unsheltered veterans experiencing homelessness on one night in January 2010 and an estimate of the number of veterans living in shelter who were homeless at any point from October 1, 2009, through September 30, 2010.[23] See **Table 1** for these estimates.

- **Point-in-Time Estimate:** The veterans supplement estimated that 76,329 veterans experienced homelessness on one night in January 2010.[24] The estimate relied on local CoC point-in-time reports with adjustments similar to those that were made in the 2009 report to account for missing data. Of the 76,329 homeless veterans, a reported 57% were sleeping in emergency shelter or transitional housing and 43% were on the street or in other places not meant for human habitation.[25]
- **HMIS Estimate:** Using data from a sample of 320 communities, researchers estimated that 144,842 veterans were homeless on at least one night from October 1, 2009, through September 30, 2010.[26] The data reported by local CoCs were adjusted to account for sheltered adults whose veteran status was unknown and for emergency shelters and transitional housing facilities that did not report data to the local HMIS.[27]

In both the point-in-time estimate and the HMIS estimate, veterans were overrepresented in the homeless population. According to the point-in-time estimate, veterans represented 16% of the adult homeless population (compared to 9.5% of the total adult population), and in the HMIS estimate veterans were about 13% of the adult homeless population.[28]

2011 Point-in-Time Estimates of Homeless Veterans

The AHAR for 2011 has not yet been released, but in December 2011, HUD released point-in-time estimates from January 2011 as a supplement to the AHAR.[29] The estimates include homeless veterans.

- **Point-in-Time Estimate:** The number of veterans estimated to be homeless on one night in January 2011 was 67,495, down from 76,329 in January of 2010. Of those who were homeless, an estimated 59% were living in shelter and 41% on the street or other place not meant for human habitation. Homeless veterans were estimated to make up 14% of the adult homeless population.

History of VA Estimates of Homeless Veterans

In every year from FY1998 through FY2009, the VA included estimates of the number of homeless veterans receiving services in its "Community Homelessness Assessment, Local Education and Networking Groups" (CHALENG) report to Congress.[30] The estimates were made as part of the CHALENG process, through which representatives from each local VA medical center called "points of contact" (POCs) coordinate with service providers from state and local governments and nonprofit organizations as well as homeless or formerly homeless veterans themselves to determine the needs of homeless veterans and plan for how best to deliver services. The FY2010 CHALENG report did not contain estimates of the number of homeless veterans, stating that the homeless veterans supplement to the AHAR would be used for "the single Federal estimate on homelessness among Veterans."[31]

The ways in which POCs estimated the number of veterans who were homeless in their area in the years prior to FY2010 varied, and most POCs used more than one source to arrive at their estimates. These included HUD point-in-time counts, VA client data, information from local homeless services providers, U.S. Census data, VA low-income population estimates, local homeless census studies, and VA staff impressions.[32]

For the first six years in which the VA released CHALENG estimates (FY1998 through FY2003), the VA asked POCs to estimate the number of veterans who were homeless *at any time during the year*, so the estimate was meant to represent the total number of veterans who experience homelessness during the course of a year. However, starting in FY2004 and continuing through the FY2009 CHALENG report, the VA changed its methodology and asked POCs from each medical center to provide estimates of the highest number of veterans who are homeless on *any given day during the year*. The new methodology was a point-in-time count and was meant to reflect the total number of veterans who might experience homelessness on a single day. The VA considered the estimates using the point-in-time methodology to be more reliable than earlier estimates.[33] From FY2007 through FY2009, the VA updated the way in which estimates were compiled in order to be more in line with HUD's point-in-time count. The VA asked POCs to estimate the number of veterans experiencing homelessness on one night during the same one-week period used in HUD point-in-time counts—the last week of January. For a summary of VA estimates since 1998, see **Table 2**.

Demographic Characteristics of Homeless Veterans

Until recently, the best data available regarding the demographics of homeless veterans preceded the wars in Iraq and Afghanistan. However, HUD and the VA, in the Veterans Supplements to the Annual Homeless Assessment Reports to Congress, include demographic data about veterans living in shelter (the data don't include information about those living on the streets or other place not meant for human habitation). In addition, characteristics about those individuals served through VA homeless programs are available from annual VA reports. Further, some of the older reports still provide comprehensive, valuable information about the homeless veteran population and may serve as a useful point of comparison to the more recent data. The next three sections present some of this information.

Table 2. VA CHALENG Estimates of Homeless Veterans

Fiscal Year	Estimate	Details of Estimates
1998	256,872	From FY1998 to FY2003, VA points of contact estimated the total number of veterans experiencing homelessness at any time during the year.
1999	344,983	
2000	292,105	
2001	294,840	
2002	299,321	
2003	313,087	
2004	192,368	In FY2004, the CHALENG report changed methodology and went from an estimate of all veterans experiencing homelessness at some point during the year to a point-in-time estimate of the highest number of veterans homeless on any given day of the year. The VA considers the recent estimates to be more reliable.
2005	194,254	
2006	195,827	
2007	153,584	
2008	131,230	
2009	106,558	

Source: VA CHALENG estimates of homeless veterans provided by the VA Office of Homeless Veterans Programs (FY1998 through FY2005) and VA CHALENG reports to Congress (FY2006 through FY2009).

Demographic Characteristics Reported in the Annual Homeless Assessment Report

The 2010 AHAR provided demographic information about veterans experiencing homelessness who were living in shelter, and who were included in local Homeless Management Information Systems (HMIS) efforts to learn more about those who are homeless.[34] The AHAR provided comparisons of veterans in the homeless population to veterans living in poverty and veterans as a percentage of the general population.

- **Gender:** Homeless veterans are predominantly men (92%), with women making up 8% of homeless veterans. Women represent 6.8% of all veterans, and 10.2% of veterans who are poor.

- **Race and Ethnicity:** African American veterans make up 35.1% of the homeless veteran population, compared to 18.9% of veterans in poverty, and 10.4% of all veterans. Hispanic veterans comprise 5.1% of homeless veterans, 4.1% of poor veterans, and 3.4% of all veterans. Non-Hispanic White veterans made up 52.1% of homeless veterans (compared to 70.3% of veterans in poverty and 81.5% of all veterans).
- **Age:** While almost half of veterans in general are age 62 and older, veterans in the 31-50 and 51-61 age groups have the greatest percentages of homeless veterans. They are each almost equally represented at 41% of the homeless veteran population. Veterans between 18 and 30 make up 8.8%, and veterans again 62 and older make up 8.6%.

Demographic Characteristics of Veterans Served in VA Homeless Programs

The VA collects data from a number of programs that serve homeless veterans on VA medical center campuses, in health clinics, and in the community. The programs include Health Care for Homeless Veterans (HCHV), Domiciliary Care for Homeless Veterans (DCHV), and the Compensated Work Therapy/Therapeutic Residences Program, all of which are described in more detail later in this report (see the section entitled "Federal Programs that Serve Homeless Veterans"). Each fiscal year, the VA publishes reports to Congress about veterans served in these programs. While the demographics of the veterans served in these programs do not constitute a representative sample of homeless veterans, and some veterans may be served in more than one program, the information may give a picture of the veterans who seek assistance and/or receive services.

Exact comparisons of the veteran population in general are not available for each demographic category, but based on available data, some differences between homeless veterans served in VA programs and veterans in general include the following:

- African American veterans are over-represented among veterans served in homeless programs, making up 11.6% of the veteran population in 2011 but representing more than 40% of those served in each program.[35]
- As previous studies have found, veterans who served in the post-Vietnam era but prior to the Gulf War era are also over-represented among those served in the VA homeless programs.[36]

- Veterans served in homeless programs have higher unemployment rates (ranging between 20% and 25%) compared to veterans in general (8.1% in 2009).[37]
- Both male and female veterans were married at a higher rate than veterans served in the VA's homeless programs—68% of men and 47% of women compared to between 5% and 7% of those served in VA programs.[38]

Table 3, below, summarizes the data.

Demographic Information from Studies Prior to the Iraq and Afghanistan Wars

Some of the more rigorous studies that have compared homeless veterans to homeless men and women who are nonveterans occurred during the 1980s and 1990s. So while these data do not include recently separated veterans who served in Iraq and Afghanistan, they provide a picture of homeless veterans during past decades, and may act as a useful comparison as more data become available about veterans who are currently homeless. According to data from several studies during the 1980s, homeless male veterans were more likely to be older and better educated than the general population of homeless men.[39] However, they were found to have more health problems than nonveteran homeless men, including AIDS, cancer, and hypertension.[40] They also suffered from mental illness and alcohol abuse at higher rates than nonveterans. A study published in 2002 found similar results regarding age and education. Homeless male veterans tended to be older, on average, than nonveteran homeless men.[41] Homeless veterans were also different in that they had reached higher levels of education than their nonveteran counterparts[42] and were more likely to be working for pay. They were also more likely to have been homeless for more than one year, and more likely to be dependent on or abuse alcohol. Family backgrounds among homeless veterans tended to be more stable, with veterans experiencing less family instability[43] and fewer incidents of conduct disorder,[44] while also being less likely to have never married than nonveteran homeless men. Homeless women veterans have also been found to have different characteristics than nonveteran homeless women. Based on data collected during the late 1990s, female veterans, like male veterans, were found to have reached higher levels of education than nonveteran homeless women, and were also more likely to have been employed in the 30 days prior to being surveyed.[45] They also had more stable family backgrounds, and lower rates of conduct disorder as children.

OVERREPRESENTATION OF VETERANS IN THE HOMELESS POPULATION

Until the advent of the Veterans Supplement to the Annual Homeless Assessment Report, research that captures information about homeless veterans had not been conducted on a regular, systematic basis. However, in addition to HUD's ongoing efforts to collect information about homeless individuals, the VA's relatively new National Center for Homelessness Among Veterans is conducting a variety of research studies. One of the studies released by the VA research center builds on earlier research about whether veterans are overrepresented in the homeless population using 2009 data from Homeless Management Information Systems (HMIS). This section discusses previous studies regarding the overrepresentation of veterans in the homeless population and the VA's more recent findings. Possibly the most comprehensive national data collection effort regarding persons experiencing homelessness prior to HMIS took place in 1996 as part of the National Survey of Homeless Assistance Providers and Clients (NSHAPC), when researchers interviewed thousands of homeless assistance providers and homeless individuals across the country.[46] Prior to the NSHAPC, in 1987, researchers from the Urban Institute surveyed nearly 2,000 homeless individuals and clients in large cities nationwide as part of a national study.[47] The data from these two surveys served as the basis for more in depth research regarding homeless veterans, but did not include veterans of the conflicts in Iraq and Afghanistan. In 2012, the VA released research using 2009 HMIS data from seven communities, called "Continuums of Care," which included veterans from the wars in Iraq and Afghanistan.[48]

Table 3. Information About Veterans Served in VA Homeless Programs, FY2009

Characteristics	Health Care for Homeless Veterans (HCHV)	Domiciliary Care for Homeless Veterans (DCHV)	Compensated Work Therapy Program/ Therapeutic Residences (CWT/TR)
Veteran Population Surveyed	40,216[a]	6,311[b]	759[c]
Average Age	50.9	49.6	48.6
Marital Status			
% Married	6.4	6.6	5.6
% Divorced/Separated/ Widowed	64.2[d]	66.1	62.0
% Never Married	29.4	27.3	32.4

Table 3. (Continued)

Characteristics	Health Care for Homeless Veterans (HCHV)	Domiciliary Care for Homeless Veterans (DCHV)	Compensated Work Therapy Program/ Therapeutic Residences (CWT/TR)
Gender			
% Men	95.4	95.1	95.4
% Women	4.6	4.9	4.6
Race/Ethnicity			
% White, Non-Hispanic	46.4	48.5	48.7
% African American	42.8	43.6	43.9
% Hispanic	7.3	5.0	3.8
% American Indian/Alaskan	1.5	1.6	—[c]
% Asian/Pacific Islander	0.9	0.5	—[c]
% Other	1.0	0.8	3.6
Era Served			
% Prior to Vietnam Era	3.2[f]	1.3[g]	0.3[h]
% Vietnam	35.9	30.6	26.0
% Post-Vietnam	43.7	50.3	53.7
% Persian Gulf (1991-Present)[i]	17.1	17.7	20.0
Employment Pattern over the Previous Three Years			
% Employed Full Time	20.6	37.2	45.8
% Employed Part Time	29.7	20.2	30.8
% Unemployed	24.4	23.0	20.1
% Retired or with Disability	23.9	18.7	2.8
% Other	1.5[j]	0.9	0.5
Mental Health and Substance Use Issues			
% Substance Use Disorder	62.1	90.2	96.4
% Serious Psychiatric Problem	54.0	67.9	59.4
% Dually Diagnosed[k]	62.1	61.0	56.5

Sources: Wesley J. Kasprow, Timothy Cuerdon, Diane DiLello, Leslie Cavallaro, and Nicole Harelik, *Healthcare for Homeless Veterans Programs: Twenty-Third Annual Report* (HCHV program report), U.S. Department of Veterans Affairs Northeast Program Evaluation Center, March 25, 2010; Catherine Leda Seibyl, Sharon Medak, Linda Baldino, and Timothy Cuerdon, *Twenty-First Progress Report on the Domiciliary Care for Homeless Veterans Program, FY2009* (DCHV program report), U.S. Department of Veterans Affairs Northeast Program Evaluation Center, March 24 2010; and Catherine Leda Seibyl, Sharon Medak, Linda Baldino, and Timothy Cuerdon, *Compensated Work Therapy/Transitional Residence (CWT/TR) Program FY2009* (CWT/TR program report), Department of Veterans Affairs, Northeast Program Evaluation Center, June 2010.

a. The HCHV program report provides demographic information on clients assessed for program participation. HCHV report, p. 24.

b. The DCHV program report provides information regarding veterans who completed treatment in the program in FY2008; the information was collected at the time of admission. DCHV report, p. 11.

c. The CWT/TR program report provides demographic information on clients admitted into the program.

d. The HCHV program report separately breaks out the percentage of veterans separated (13.5%), divorced (46.6%), and widowed (4.1%).

e. This information is not provided.

f. For the HCHV program, the line showing the percentage of veterans serving prior to the Vietnam era aggregates five eras: pre-WWII (0.2%), WWII (0.2%), pre-Korea (0.1%), Korea (0.7%), and pre-Vietnam (2.0%). See HCHV report, p. 46.

g. For the DCHV program, the line showing the percentage of veterans serving prior to the Vietnam era aggregates four eras: WWII (0.0%), pre-Korea (0.0%), Korea (0.2%), and pre-Vietnam (1.1%). See DCHV report, p. 37.

h. For the CWT/TR program, the line showing the percentage of veterans serving prior to the Vietnam era aggregates two eras: Korea (0.0%) and pre-Vietnam (0.3%).

i. Each of the three programs use intake forms that specify the Persian Gulf Era as August 1990 to the present. See HCHV program report, p. 314; DCHV program report, p. 19; and the CWT program report, p. 15.

j. The HCHV program report categorizes those assessed as student/service.

k. Dual diagnosis refers to having both a substance use disorder and a serious psychiatric diagnosis.

Results from a total of five studies are presented here. The studies all looked at veterans as a percentage of the general population compared to veterans as a percentage of the homeless population and determined the likelihood of veterans to be homeless compared to non-veterans. The data in each of the studies relied on samples of homeless individuals, and adjustments were made for such factors as age and race.

In each of the studies, both male and female veterans were more likely to be homeless than their nonveteran counterparts.[49] This was not always the case, however.

Although veterans have always been present among the homeless population, the studies from the 1980s and 1990s found that cohorts serving in the Vietnam[50] and post-Vietnam eras were overrepresented while veterans of World War II and Korea were less likely to be homeless than their nonveteran counterparts.[51] The VA study using 2009 HMIS data also found that Vietnam and post-Vietnam veterans were overrepresented.

Overrepresentation of Male Veterans

Two earlier national studies—one published in 1994 using data from the 1987 Urban Institute survey (as well as data from surveys in Los Angeles, Baltimore, and Chicago), and the other published in 2001 using data from the 1996 NSHAPC—found that male veterans were overrepresented in the homeless population.

In addition, researchers in both studies determined that the likelihood of homelessness depended on the ages of veterans.[52] During both periods of time, the odds of a veteran being homeless were highest for veterans who had enlisted after the military transitioned to an all-volunteer force (AVF) in 1973. These veterans were age 20-34 at the time of the first study, and age 35-44 at the time of the second study.

In the first study, researchers found that 41% of adult homeless men were veterans, compared to just under 34% of adult males in the general population. Overall, male veterans were 1.4 times as likely to be homeless as nonveterans.[53] Notably, though, those veterans who served after the Vietnam War were four times more likely to be homeless than nonveterans in the same age group.[54]

Vietnam era veterans, who are often thought to be the most overrepresented group of homeless veterans, were barely more likely to be homeless than nonveterans (1.01 times). (See **Table 4** for a breakdown of the likelihood of homelessness based on age.)

In the second study, researchers found that nearly 33% of adult homeless men were veterans, compared to 28% of males in the general population. Once again, the likelihood of homelessness differed among age groups. Overall, male veterans were 1.25 times more likely to be homeless than nonveterans.[55] However, the same post-Vietnam cohort as that in the 1994 study was most at risk of homelessness; those veterans in the cohort were over three times as likely to be homeless as nonveterans in the same cohort. Younger veterans, those age 20-34 in 1996, were two times as likely to be homeless as nonveterans.

And Vietnam era veterans were approximately 1.4 times as likely to be homeless as their nonveteran counterparts. (See **Table 4**.)

The study produced by the VA using 2009 HMIS data from seven jurisdictions similarly found higher rates of homelessness for male veterans than their presence in the general population would indicate (13.6% of homeless adult men were veterans compared to 13.4% of the general population), and that they were 1.3 times more likely to be homeless than males generally. In addition, the study noted similar cohort effects to the earlier research. Veterans age 45-54, those who served in the early years of the AVF, were generally at a higher risk of homelessness compared to male veterans in other cohorts—African American veterans age 45-54 were 1.4 times more likely to be homeless, and non-Black veterans were 2.0 times as likely to be homeless as their nonveteran counterparts.[56]

Table 4 contains results from the VA study, broken down by age, race, and gender.

Overrepresentation of Female Veterans

As with male veterans, research has shown that women veterans are more likely to be homeless than women who are not veterans. A study published in 2003 examined two data sources, one a survey of mentally ill homeless women, and the other the NSHAPC, and found that 4.4% and 3.1% of those homeless persons surveyed were female veterans, respectively (compared to approximately 1.3% of the general population).[57]

Although the likelihood of homelessness was different for each of the two surveyed populations, the study estimated that female veterans were between two and four times as likely to be homeless as their nonveteran counterparts.[58]

Unlike male veterans, all birth cohorts were more likely to be homeless than nonveterans. However, with the exception of women veterans age 35-55 (representing the post-Vietnam era), who were between approximately 3.5 and 4.0 times as likely to be homeless as nonveterans, cohort data were not consistent between the two surveys. (See **Table 4** for a breakdown of likelihood of homelessness by cohort.)

The VA study that used 2009 HMIS data to determine the likelihood of homelessness among veterans contains more detailed data on women veterans, including risk of homelessness broken down by age and race (Black and non-Black). All women veterans, regardless of age or race, face an increased risk of homelessness, according to the study.

Overall, women veterans are 2.1 times more likely to be homeless than their nonveteran counterparts.[59] While women veterans of older ages were more likely to be homeless than their age-group counterparts, researchers found that, in general, younger women veterans, especially African American women, were more likely to be homeless than older women veterans.[60]

Table 4. Results from Five Studies: Veterans as a Percentage of the Homeless Population and Likelihood of Experiencing Homelessness

Veteran Group	Veterans as a Percentage of the General Population[a]	Veterans as a Percentage of the Homeless Population	Odds Ratio (Likelihood of Homelessness among Veterans vs. Nonveterans)
Men (data 1986-1987)[b]	33.6	41.2	1.38
Age 20-34	10.0	30.6	3.95
Age 35-44	36.9	37.2	1.01
Age 45-54	44.8	58.7	1.75
Age 55-64	69.9	61.7	0.69
Age 65 and Older	46.3	37.4	0.71
Men (data 1996)[c]	28.0	32.7	1.25
Age 20-34	7.7	14.5	2.04
Age 35-44	13.8	33.7	3.17
Age 45-54	38.4	46.5	1.39
Age 55-64	48.7	45.8	0.89[f]
Age 65 and Older	62.6	59.5	0.88[f]
Non-Black Men (data 2009)[g]	13.6	13.4	1.3
Age 18-29	2.1	2.7	1.3
Age 30-44	5.9	7.6	1.3
Age 45-54	9.8	19.6	2.0
Age 55-64	27.6	30.6	1.1
Age 65 and Older	45.4	33.7	0.7
Black Men (data 2009)[g]	11.8	13.7	1.4
Age 18-29	1.9	3.8	2.0
Age 30-44	7.3	8.2	1.1
Age 45-54	14.7	21.0	1.4
Age 55-64	23.0	31.9	1.4
Age 65 and Older	33.2	32.3	1.0
Women (data 1994-1998)[d]	1.3	4.4	3.58
Age 20-34	—	—	3.61
Age 35-44	—	—	3.48
Age 45-54	—	—	4.42
Age 55 and Older	—	—	1.54[f]
Women (data 1996)[c]	1.2	3.1	2.71
Age 20-34	—	—	1.60[f]
Age 35-44	—	—	3.98
Age 45-54	—	—	2.00[f]
Age 55 and Older	—	—	4.40
Non-Black Women (data 2009)[g]	0.9	1.6	2.1
Age 18-29	0.5	1.0	2.0
Age 30-44	0.8	1.3	1.6
Age 45-54	1.2	3.1	2.5

Veteran Group	Veterans as a Percentage of the General Population[a]		Veterans as a Percentage of the Homeless Population		Odds Ratio (Likelihood of Homelessness among Veterans vs. Nonveterans)	
Age 55-64		1.0		3.1		3.1
Age 65 and Older		1.1		2.4		2.1
Black Women (data 2009)[e]	1.1		2.0		1.9	
Age 18-29		0.6		1.0		1.7
Age 30-44		1.6		3.2		1.9
Age 45-54		1.7		2.7		1.6
Age 55-64		0.9		1.8		1.9
Age 65 and Older		0.6		1.4		2.6

Sources: Robert Rosenheck, Linda Frisman, and An-Me Chung, "The Proportion of Veterans Among Homeless Men," *American Journal of Public Health* 84, no. 3 (March 1994): 466-469; Gail Gamache, Robert Rosenheck, and Richard Tessler, "The Proportion of Veterans Among Homeless Men: A Decade Later," *Social Psychiatry and Psychiatric Epidemiology* 36, no. 10 (October 2001): 481-485; Gail Gamache, Robert Rosenheck, and Richard Tessler, "Overrepresentation of Women Veterans Among Homeless Women," *American Journal of Public Health* 93, no. 7 (July 2003): 1132-1136; and Jamison Fargo, Stephen Metraux, and Thomas Byrne, et al., "Prevalence and Risk of Homelessness Among U.S. Veterans," *Preventing Chronic Disease*, vol. 9 (January 26, 2012), http://www.cdc.gov/pcd/issues/2012/11_0112.htm.

a. Data are from the Current Population Survey.

b. Data are from the Urban Institute Study and three community surveys conducted between 1985 and 1987.

c. Data are from the National Survey of Homeless Assistance Providers and Clients (NSHAPC).

d. Data are from the Access to Community Care and Effective Services and Supports sample of women with mental illness.

e. Data are from the NSHAPC.

f. Not statistically significant.

g. Data are from the American Community Survey and from seven Continuums of Care: New York City; San Jose/Santa Clara County, CA; Columbus/Franklin County, OH; Denver, CO; Tampa/Hillsborough County, FL; Phoenix/Maricopa County, AZ; and Lansing/Ingham County, MI.

Why Are Veterans Overrepresented in the Homeless Population?

While data collection regarding the number and prevalence of veterans in the homeless population has become robust, information about why homeless veterans are more likely to be homeless than nonveterans is less investigated. The recent VA report about the risk and prevalence of homelessness among veterans noted that

> The presence of additional risk for homelessness specifically associated with Veteran status is puzzling in that it occurs among a population that shows better outcomes on almost all socioeconomic measures and that has exclusive access to an extensive system of benefits that include comprehensive healthcare services, disability and pension assistance, and homeless services. Explanations to account for this risk go beyond the basic demographic factors explained here, and underscore the need for identifying other correlates of homelessness among the Veteran population as the basis for prevention efforts.[61]

While researchers have attempted to explain why veterans are homeless in higher proportions than their numbers in the general population, as with some of the studies already discussed in this report, findings are somewhat dated and do not include veterans of Iraq and Afghanistan. However, previous research, which has found that factors present both prior to military service and those that developed during or after service are associated with veterans' homelessness, could also be applicable to today's returning veterans.

Most of the evidence about factors associated with homelessness among veterans comes from The National Vietnam Veterans Readjustment Study (NVVRS) conducted from 1984 to 1988.[62] Researchers for the NVVRS surveyed 1,600 Vietnam theater veterans (those serving in Vietnam, Cambodia, or Laos) and 730 Vietnam era veterans (who did not serve in the theater) to determine their mental health status and their ability to readjust to civilian life. The NVVRS did not specifically analyze homelessness. However, a later study, published in 1994, used data from the NVVRS to examine homelessness specifically.[63] Findings from both studies are discussed below.

Factors Present during and after Military Service

Although researchers have not found that military service alone is associated with homelessness,[64] it may be associated with other factors that contribute to homelessness. The NVVRS found an indirect connection between the stress that occurs as a result of deployment and exposure to combat, or "war-zone stress," and homelessness. Vietnam theater and era veterans who experienced war-zone stress were found to have difficulty readjusting to civilian life, resulting in higher levels of problems that included social isolation, violent behavior, and, for white male veterans, homelessness.[65]

The 1994 study of Vietnam era veterans (hereinafter referred to as the Rosenheck/Fontana study) evaluated 18 variables that could be associated with homelessness. The study categorized each variable in one of four groups according to when they occurred in the veteran's life: pre-military, military, the one-year readjustment period, and the post-military period subsequent to readjustment.[66] Variables from each time period were found to be associated with homelessness, although their effects varied. The two military factors— combat exposure and participation in atrocities—did not have a direct relationship to homelessness. However, those two factors did contribute to (1) low levels of social support upon returning home, (2) psychiatric disorders (not including Post Traumatic Stress Disorder (PTSD)), (3) substance use disorders, and (4) being unmarried (including separation and divorce). Each of these four post-military variables, in turn, contributed directly to homelessness.[67] In fact, social isolation, measured by low levels of support in the first year after discharge from military service, together with the status of being unmarried, had the strongest association with homelessness of the 18 factors examined in the study.[68]

Post-Traumatic Stress Disorder (PTSD)

Researchers examining factors related to homelessness have not found a direct relationship between PTSD and homelessness. The Rosenheck/Fontana study "found no unique association between combat-related PTSD and homelessness."[69] An unrelated study determined that homeless combat veterans were no more likely to be diagnosed with PTSD than combat veterans who were not homeless.[70] However, the NVVRS found that PTSD was significantly related to other psychiatric disorders, substance abuse, problems in interpersonal relationships, and unemployment.[71] These conditions can lead to readjustment difficulties and are considered risk factors for homelessness.[72]

Factors that Pre-date Military Service

According to research, factors that predate military service also play a role in homelessness among veterans. The Rosenheck/Fontana study found that three variables present in the lives of veterans before they joined the military had a significant direct relationship to homelessness. These were exposure to physical or sexual abuse prior to age 18; exposure to other traumatic experiences, such as experiencing a serious accident or natural disaster, or seeing someone killed; and placement in foster care prior to age 16.[73] The researchers also found that a history of conduct disorder had a substantial indirect effect on homelessness.[74] Conduct disorder includes behaviors such as being suspended or expelled from school, involvement with law enforcement, or having poor academic performance. Another pre-military variable that might contribute to homelessness among veterans is a lack of family support prior to enlistment.[75]

The conditions present in the lives of veterans prior to military service, and the growth of homelessness among veterans, have been tied to the institution of the all volunteer force (AVF) in 1973. As discussed earlier in this report, the overrepresentation of veterans in the homeless population is most prevalent in the birth cohort that joined the military after the Vietnam War. It is possible that higher rates of homelessness among these veterans are due to "lowered recruitment standards during periods where military service was not held in high regard."[76] Individuals who joined the military during the time after the implementation of the AVF might have been more likely to have characteristics that are risk factors for homelessness.[77]

FEDERAL PROGRAMS THAT SERVE HOMELESS VETERANS

The federal response to the needs of homeless veterans, like the federal response to homelessness generally, began in the late 1980s. Congress, aware of the data showing that veterans were disproportionately represented among homeless persons,[78] began to hold hearings and enact legislation in the late 1980s. Among the programs enacted were Health Care for Homeless Veterans, Domiciliary Care for Homeless Veterans, and the Homeless Veterans Reintegration Program. Also around this time, the first national group dedicated to the cause of homeless veterans, the National Coalition for Homeless Veterans, was founded by service providers that were concerned about the growing number of homeless veterans.

While homeless veterans are eligible for and receive services through programs that are not designed specifically for homeless veterans, the VA funds multiple programs to serve homeless veterans. The majority of homeless programs are run through the Veterans Health Administration (VHA), which administers health care programs for veterans.[79] The Veterans Benefits Administration (VBA), which is responsible for compensation and pensions,[80] education assistance,[81] home loan guarantees,[82] and insurance, operates one program for homeless veterans. In addition, the Department of Labor (DOL) is responsible for programs that provide employment services for homeless veterans while the Department of Housing and Urban Development (HUD) collaborates with the VA on two additional programs. Many of these programs are summarized in this section.

The Department of Veterans Affairs

The majority of programs that serve homeless veterans are part of the Veterans Health Administration (VHA), one of the three major organizations within the VA (the other two are the Veterans Benefits Administration (VBA) and the National Cemetery Administration).[83] The VHA operates hospitals and outpatient clinics across the country through 21 Veterans Integrated Service Networks (VISNs). Each VISN oversees between five and eleven VA hospitals as well as outpatient clinics, nursing homes, and domiciliary care facilities. In all, there are 157 VA hospitals, 750 outpatient clinics, 134 nursing homes, and 42 domiciliary care facilities across the country. Many services for homeless veterans are provided in these facilities. In addition, the VBA has made efforts to coordinate with the VHA regarding homeless veterans by placing Homeless Veteran Outreach Coordinators (HVOCs) in its offices in order to assist homeless veterans in their applications for benefits.

Health Care for Homeless Veterans

The first federal program to specifically address the needs of homeless veterans, Health Care for Homeless Veterans (HCHV), was initially called the Homeless Chronically Mentally Ill veterans program.[84] The program was created as part of an emergency appropriations act for FY1987 (P.L. 100-6) in which Congress allocated $5 million to the VA to provide medical and psychiatric care in community-based facilities to homeless veterans suffering from mental illness.[85] Through the HCHV program, VA medical center staff conduct outreach to homeless veterans, provide care and treatment for medical, psychiatric, and substance use disorders, and refer veterans to other needed supportive services.[86] Although P.L. 100-6 provided priority for veterans whose illnesses were service-connected, veterans with non-service-connected disabilities were also made eligible for the program. Within two months of the program's enactment, 43 VA Medical Centers had initiated programs to find and assist mentally ill homeless veterans.[87] Currently, 132 VA sites have implemented HCHV programs.[88] The HCHV program is authorized through December 31, 2012.[89]

Program Data

The HCHV program itself does not provide housing for veterans who receive services. However, the VA was initially authorized to enter into contracts with non-VA service providers to place veterans in residential treatment facilities so that they would have a place to stay while receiving treatment. In FY2003, the VA shifted funding from contracts with residential treatment facilities to the VA Grant and Per Diem program (described later in this section).[90] Local funding for residential treatment facilities continues to be provided by some VA medical center locations, however. According to data from the VA, 2,472 veterans stayed in residential treatment facilities in FY2009, with an average stay of about 68 days.[91] The HCHV program as a whole treated approximately 77,696 veterans in that same year.[92]

Of veterans screened for admission to HCHV, 54% had a severe psychiatric problem, about 60% were dependent on alcohol and/or drugs, and 37% had both a psychiatric problem and a substance use disorder.[93] Housing outcomes reported for veterans who lived in residential treatment facilities were as follows: 37.6% of residents moved into an apartment, room, or house (unspecified whether on their own or shared with another); 36.7% moved into a halfway house or other transitional housing; 8.2% did not identify a housing situation; and the whereabouts of another 17.5% were unknown.[94] Regarding employment, 16.1% of those who left residential treatment facilities were engaged in full- or part-time employment, 14.3% were involved in veterans industries, 29.6% had a disability or were retired, and 34.2% were unemployed. The outcomes include veterans who are considered to have both successful and unsuccessful discharges from the program. Successful discharge is one where "the discharge was mutually agreed-upon and the Veteran participated in accordance with program rules and treatment goals."[95] See **Table 5**.

Domiciliary Care for Homeless Veterans

Domiciliary care consists of rehabilitative services for physically and mentally ill or aged veterans who need assistance, but are not in need of the level of care offered by hospitals and nursing homes. Congress first provided funds for the Domiciliary Care program for homeless veterans in 1987 through a supplemental appropriations act (P.L. 100-71). Prior to enactment of P.L. 100-71, domiciliary care for veterans generally (now often referred to as Residential Rehabilitation and Treatment programs) had existed since the 1860s. The program for homeless veterans was implemented to reduce the use of more expensive inpatient treatment, improve health status, and reduce the likelihood of homelessness through employment and other assistance. Congress has appropriated funds for the DCHV program since its inception.

Program Data

The DCHV program operates at 42 VA medical centers and has 2,152 beds available.[96] In FY2009, the number of veterans completing treatment was 6,311.[97] Of those admitted to DCHV programs, 90.2% were diagnosed with a substance use disorder, more than two-thirds (67.9%) were diagnosed with serious mental illness, and 61.0% had both diagnoses.[98] The average length of stay for veterans in FY2009 was 112 days, during which they received medical, psychiatric, and substance abuse treatment, as well as vocational rehabilitation. Upon discharge, the VA reported that 30.5% of veterans went to live in their own apartment, room, or house; 25.1% moved in with a family member or friend; 26.7% continued treatment in a halfway house, transitional housing program, nursing home, or another domiciliary program; 5.8% were homeless upon discharge; 1.1% were discharged to jail or prison; and the location of 7.7% of participants was unknown.[99] In the area of employment, 22.0% of veterans were in part- or full-time employment, 23.6% had a disability or were retired, 25.0% were unemployed, and 19.0% were engaged in vocational training or the VA's Compensated Work Therapy program. See **Table 5**.

Compensated Work Therapy/Transitional Residence Program

The Compensated Work Therapy (CWT) Program has existed at the VA in some form since the 1930s.[100] The program was authorized in P.L. 87-574 as "Therapeutic and Rehabilitative Activities," and was substantially amended in P.L. 94-581, an act that amended various aspects of veteran health care programs.[101] The CWT program is permanently authorized through the VA's Special Therapeutic and Rehabilitation Activities Fund.[102]

The goal of the CWT program is to give veterans with disabilities work experience and skills so that they may re-enter the workforce and maintain employment on their own. The VA either employs veterans directly (in FY2009, 47.6% of veterans in the CWT program worked for the VA[103]), finds work for veterans at other federal agencies, or enters into contracts with private companies or nonprofit organizations that then provide veterans with work opportunities. Veterans must be paid wages commensurate with those wages in the community for similar work, and through the experience the goal is that participants will improve their chances of living independently and reaching self sufficiency. In 2003, the Veterans Health Care, Capital Asset, and Business Improvement Act (P.L. 108-170) added work skills training, employment support services, and job development and placement services to the activities authorized by the CWT program.

In 1991, as part of P.L. 102-54, the Veterans Housing, Memorial Affairs, and Technical Amendments Act, Congress added the Therapeutic Transitional Housing component to the CWT program. The housing component is authorized through December 31, 2012.[104] The purpose of the program is to provide housing to participants in the CWT program who have mental illnesses or chronic substance use disorders and who are homeless or at risk of homelessness.[105] Although the law initially provided that both the VA itself or private nonprofit organizations, through contracts with the VA, could operate housing, the law was subsequently changed so that only the VA now owns and operates housing.[106] The housing is transitional—up to 12 months—and veterans who reside there receive supportive services. As of FY2009, the VA operated 42 transitional housing facilities with 633 beds.[107]

Program Data

In FY2009, 11,385 veterans were admitted into the CWT program, 52% of whom were homeless. Similar to those veterans who enter into the VA's Health Care for Homeless Veterans and Domiciliary Care for Homeless Veterans programs, large percentages of veterans engaged in the CWT program in FY2009 suffered from mental illness and substance abuse issues. Of those admitted to the CWT program, 72.9% of veterans had a substance abuse problem, 67.5% had serious mental illness, and 46.6% were dually diagnosed (i.e., had both a substance abuse issue and mental illness).[108] In addition, 80.1% of participants were found to have a disabling medical condition, with nearly all participants (99.8%) having a psychiatric disorder or disabling medical condition or both.[109]

Of those who were discharged from the program (10,895 veterans), more than half (53.7%) left through a mutually agreed upon or planned discharge.[110] 27.3% were in full or part-time employment.[111] Approximately 13.2% were involved in activities including training, volunteering, interning, or continuing in VA-supported work; 16.1% retired or were considered disabled; and 43.2% were unemployed.[112] The reported housing situations of those discharged from the program were as follows: 43.0% were living in their own apartment, house, or room; 19.5% were living with family or friends; another 19.5% were in transitional housing or a halfway house; 3.3% were in a nursing home or domiciliary facility; 4.1% had no available residence, and the location of the remaining participants (10.6%) was unknown.[113] See **Table 5**.

Grant and Per Diem Program

Initially called the Comprehensive Service Programs, the Grant and Per Diem program was introduced as a pilot program in 1992 through the Homeless Veterans Comprehensive Services Act (P.L. 102-590). The law establishing the Grant and Per Diem program, which was made permanent in the Homeless Veterans Comprehensive Services Act of 2001 (P.L. 107-95), authorizes the VA to make grants to public entities or private nonprofit organizations to provide services and transitional housing to homeless veterans.[114]

The Grant and Per Diem program had been permanently authorized at $150 million (P.L. 110-387). However, as part of the Veterans Health Care Facilities Capital Improvement Act of 2011 (P.L. 112-37), Congress increased the authorization level to $175 million for FY2010, $218 million for FY2011, and $250 million for FY2012. The higher authorization levels comport with amounts that the VA estimates are needed for the program in each of the three fiscal years.[115] Beginning in FY2013 and thereafter, P.L. 112-37 provides that the authorization level will return to $150 million.

The program has two parts: grant and per diem. Eligible grant recipients may apply for funding for one or both parts. The grants portion provides capital grants to purchase, rehabilitate, or convert facilities so that they are suitable for use as either service centers or transitional housing facilities. The capital grants will fund up to 65% of the costs of acquisition, expansion or remodeling of facilities.[116] Grants may also be used to procure vans for outreach and transportation of homeless veterans. The per diem portion of the program reimburses grant recipients for the costs of providing housing and supportive services to homeless veterans. The supportive services that grantees may provide include outreach activities, food and nutrition services, health care, mental health services, substance abuse counseling, case management, child care, assistance in obtaining housing, employment counseling, job training and placement services, and transportation assistance.[117] Organizations may apply for per diem funds alone (without capital grant funds), as long as they would be eligible to apply for and receive capital grants.

Program Rules and Data

The per diem portion of the Grant and Per Diem program pays organizations for the housing and services that they provide to veterans at a fixed dollar rate for each bed that is occupied.[118] Organizations apply to be reimbursed for the cost of care provided, not to exceed the current per diem rate for domiciliary care. The per diem rate increases periodically; the current rate is $38.90 per day.[119] The per diem portion of the program also compensates grant recipients for the services they provide to veterans at service centers. Grantee organizations are paid at an hourly rate of one-eighth of either the cost of services or the domiciliary care per diem rate. Any per diem payments are offset by other funds that the grant recipient receives, so the per diem program can be thought of as a payer of last resort, covering expenses after grantees have used funds from other sources. The Advisory Committee on Homeless Veterans has recommended that the per diem reimbursement system be revised to take account of service costs and geographic disparities instead of using a capped rate, and to allow use of other funds (such as those authorized under the McKinney-Vento Homeless Assistance Grants) without offset.[120]

According to VA data, more than 400 Grant and Per Diem programs were funded in FY2009. These providers had a total of 11,645 beds available for veterans and admitted 17,008 veterans during the fiscal year.[121] Veterans stayed an average of 172 days in Grant and Per Diem transitional housing.[122] The maximum amount of time a veteran may remain in housing is 24 months, with three total stays, though clients may stay longer "if permanent housing for the veteran has not been located or if the veteran requires additional time to prepare for independent living."[123] Majorities of veterans admitted into the program and later discharged during FY2009 reported alcohol problems (72.5%), drug problems (64.4%), and mental illness (72.9%).[124] Of all the veterans who received treatment through the program, 46% of treatment episodes were considered successful, meaning that veterans "actively participated in accordance with treatment goals."[125] Of those discharged, 52.5% were living in an apartment, room, or house,[126] and 26.2% had full- or part-time employment.[127] See **Table 5**.

Grant and Per Diem for Homeless Veterans with Special Needs

In 2001, Congress created a demonstration program to target grant and per diem funds to specific groups of veterans (P.L. 107-95). These groups include women, women with children, the frail elderly, those veterans with terminal illnesses, and those with chronic mental illnesses. The program was initially authorized at $5 million per year for FY2003 through FY2005. The Special Needs grants have continued to be authorized at $5 million through FY2012, most recently as part of the Veterans Health Care Facilities Capital Improvement Act of 2011 (P.L. 112-37).

Supportive Services for Veteran Families

In the 110th Congress, the Veterans' Mental Health and Other Care Improvements Act of 2008 (P.L. 110-387) authorized a program of supportive services to assist very low-income veterans and their families who either are making the transition from homelessness to housing or who are moving from one location to another. The law specified that funds be made available for the new program from the amount appropriated for VA medical services—$15 million for FY2009, $20 million for FY2010, and $25 million for FY2011. Entities eligible for funds are private nonprofit organizations and consumer cooperatives, and funds are made available through a competitive process. Those organizations that assist families transitioning from homelessness to permanent housing are given priority for funding under the law. Among the eligible services that recipient organizations may provide are case management, health care services, daily living services, assistance with financial planning, transportation, legal assistance, child care, and housing counseling. The first grants awarded under the program were announced on July 26, 2011, with $60 million distributed to 85 nonprofit organizations in 40 states and the District of Columbia.[128] The VA released the Notice of Funding Availability for FY2011 in December 2011, with an additional $100 million available for new grants and to renew existing grants.[129] In addition, the Veterans Health Care Facilities Capital Improvement Act of 2011(P.L. 112-37), signed by the President on October 5, 2011, authorized the program through FY2012 at $100 million.

Enhanced Use Leases

Since 1991, the VA has had the authority to enter into leases with homeless service providers (among others organizations) to use VA property for a period of time. The arrangement, called Enhanced Use Leases (EULs), was made possible as part of the Veterans' Benefits Programs Improvement Act (P.L. 102-86).[130] Generally, the VA may enter into a lease that furthers the mission of the VA and enhances the use of the property or that would result in the improvement of medical care and services to veterans in the geographic area.[131] The lease may last for up to 75 years, and the VA must charge "fair consideration" for the lease, which may include in-kind payment such as goods and services that benefit the VA as well as improvements to and maintenance of VA facilities.[132] According to VA budget documents, of the 60 EULs that have been awarded, 16 are classified as homeless services, transitional housing, or single room occupancy housing,[133] while several additional projects to serve homeless veterans are approved priority projects.[134] Further, as part of the Building Utilization Review and Repurposing (BURR) Initiative, the VA identified an additional 34 properties suitable for use as transitional or permanent housing for homeless veterans in which it will enter into EULs.[135]

Table 5. Selected Outcomes for Veterans Served in VA Homeless Programs FY2009

Outcomes	Health Care for Homeless Veterans (HCHV)	Domiciliary Care for Homeless Veterans[a] (DCHV)	Compensated Work Therapy Program (CWT)	Grant and Per Diem Program (GPD)
Veteran Population Surveyed	2,463[b]	6,311[c]	10,895[d]	15,906[e]
Housing Outcomes				
% Apartment, Room, House	37.6	55.6	62.5	52.5
Own Housing	—	30.5	43.0	—
Family or Friend	—	25.1	19.5	—
% Halfway House/Transitional Housing	36.7	20.7	19.5	19.5
% Hospital, Nursing Home, Domiciliary Care	—	6.0[f]	3.3	—
% None Identified	8.2	5.8[g]	4.1	7.5
% Prison or Jail	—	1.1	—	—
% Unknown	17.5	7.7	10.6	20.6
Employment Outcomes				
% Full-Time Employment	8.9	17.9	21.3	18.8
% Part-Time Employment	7.2	4.1	6.0	7.4
% Veterans Industries/CWT	14.3[h]	18.1	5.7[i]	—
% Retired or with Disability	29.6	23.6	16.1	32.3
% Unemployed	34.2	25.0	43.2	28.3
% Training, Volunteer, Student	0.6	2.4	7.5	6.3
% Unknown	5.3[j]	6.9	15.5	6.9

Source: *Healthcare for Homeless Veterans Programs: Twenty-Third Annual Report*, Table 4-9 (HCHV) and Table 5-11 (GPD), *Twenty-First Progress Report on the Domiciliary Care for Homeless Veterans Program*, FY2009, Table 9; and *Thirteenth Progress Report on the Compensated Work Therapy (CWT) Program*, Table 6.

a. In both housing and employment outcomes, the DCHV report is the only one of the four to contain an "other" category. For housing, this category was 3.1% of the total, and for employment it was 2.2%.

b. HCHV program outcomes are for veterans who resided in residential treatment facilities.

c. DCHV outcomes are for veterans who were discharged from the program.

d. The CWT program reports outcomes for individuals discharged from the program.

e. Those in the GPD program include all individuals discharged.

f. The DCHV further breaks this information down into those discharged to hospitals or nursing homes (3.4%) and those who enter another domiciliary care program (2.6%).

g. DCHV reports this category as "shelter/outdoors."

h. HCHV refers to veterans working in "veterans industries."

i. For the CWT program, this category is for veterans engaged in the Incentive Therapy program.

j. HCHV includes "other" with unknown employment outcome.

Acquired Property Sales for Homeless Veterans

The Acquired Property Sales for Homeless Veterans program is operated through the Veterans Benefits Administration (VBA). The program was enacted as part of the Veterans Home Loan Guarantee and Property Rehabilitation Act of 1987 (P.L. 100-198). The current version of the program was authorized in P.L. 102-54 (a bill to amend Title 38 of the U.S. Code), and is authorized through December 31, 2012.[136]

Through the program, the VA is able to dispose of properties that it has acquired through foreclosures on its loans so that they can be used for the benefit of homeless veterans. Specifically, the VA can sell, lease, lease with the option to buy, or donate, properties to nonprofit organizations and state government agencies that will use the property only as homeless shelters primarily for veterans and their families.

VA and HUD Collaborations

HUD-VASH

The HUD-VA Supported Housing (HUD-VASH) program began in 1992 as a collaboration between the VA and HUD whereby HUD provided housing to homeless veterans through a set-aside of Section 8 vouchers and the VA provided supportive services. The program targeted veterans with severe psychiatric or substance use disorders and distributed approximately 1,753 Section 8 vouchers to veterans over three years.[137] Through the program, local Public Housing Authorities (PHAs) administered the Section 8 vouchers while local VA medical centers provided case management and clinical services to participating veterans. After the initial voucher distributions, no new vouchers were made available to homeless veterans for approximately 15 years—until FY2008, when HUD-VASH was revived by Congress. This section of the report discusses the program's progression.

HUD initially distributed Section 8 vouchers to PHAs through three competitions, in 1992, 1993, and 1994. Prior to issuing the vouchers, HUD and the VA had identified medical centers with Domiciliary Care and Health Care for Homeless Veterans programs that were best suited to providing services. PHAs within the geographic areas of the VA medical centers were invited to apply for vouchers. In the first year that HUD issued vouchers, 19 PHAs were eligible to apply, and by the third year the list of eligible VA medical centers and PHAs had expanded to 87.[138] HUD has not separately tracked these Section 8 vouchers, and over the years, when veterans have left the program and returned their vouchers to PHAs, the vouchers are not necessarily turned over to other veterans. The VA keeps statistics on veterans with vouchers who receive treatment through the VA, however. In FY2008, the VA reported that there were 522 veterans actively enrolled in HUD-VASH.[139]

In 2001, Congress codified the HUD-VASH program (P.L. 107-95) and authorized the creation of an additional 500 vouchers for each year from FY2003 through FY2006.[140] A bill enacted at the end of the 109th Congress (P.L. 109-461) also provided the authorization for additional HUD-VASH vouchers. However, it was not until FY2008 that Congress provided funding for additional vouchers: the Consolidated Appropriations Act (P.L. 110-161) included $75 million to fund Section 8 vouchers for homeless veterans for one year (after the first year, funding for the vouchers is absorbed into the tenant-based Section 8 account). Congress continued to fund new vouchers in FY2009 (P.L. 111-8), FY2010 (P.L. 111-117), FY2011 (P.L. 112-10), and FY2012 (P.L. 112-55) as well, appropriating $75 million in both FY2009 and FY20010, $50 million in FY2011, and another $75 million in FY2012. Language in each of the appropriations acts specified that the VA and HUD would determine the allocation of vouchers based on geographic need as determined by the VA, PHA administrative performance, and other factors that HUD and the VA may specify. Each law also provided that the vouchers must be given to another veteran upon turnover.

The appropriations laws for HUD-VASH allow HUD to waive any statutory or regulatory provision regarding the vouchers[141] if it is necessary for the "effective delivery and administration" of assistance. Pursuant to this provision, in the guidance governing the FY2008 funds for vouchers, HUD waived the statutory requirement that vouchers be made available only to those veterans with mental illnesses and substance use disorders.[142] In administering the vouchers, local VA medical centers determine veteran eligibility for the program and veterans are then referred to partnering PHAs. The PHAs review applicants only for income eligibility and to ensure that they are not subject to lifetime sex offender registration.

The FY2008 and FY2009 appropriations funded 10,150 and 10,290 new vouchers, respectively, and were distributed to recipient housing authorities located in all 50 states, the District of Columbia, Puerto Rico, and Guam.[143] In FY2010, HUD announced four separate distributions of HUD-VASH vouchers; three of the distributions were made through VA and HUD consultation, while the fourth distribution was a competitive process for project-based vouchers (described in the next section). On June 3, 2010, HUD announced the allocation of 7,705 vouchers to PHAs in 48 states, the District of Columbia, and Guam (Hawaii and Wyoming were not part of the first distribution).[144] Two weeks later, HUD announced that another 1,255 vouchers would be distributed to PHAs in 19 states (including Hawaii and Wyoming) and Puerto Rico.[145] The third round of funding was announced on September 28, 2010, with PHAs in 19 states receiving funding sufficient to support 550 vouchers.[146] Most recently, HUD announced the distribution of 6,790 vouchers funded through the FY2011 appropriation; vouchers are to be distributed to all 50 states and the District of Columbia.[147] According to the VA, as of November 2011, 27,500 vouchers were under lease, with another 5,200 veterans undergoing program approval or searching for housing.[148]

Project-Based HUD-VASH Vouchers

HUD allows PHAs to project base their HUD-VASH vouchers. When vouchers are project based, they are attached to a specific unit of housing and do not move when the tenant moves. This may be desirable in housing markets where it is difficult to find housing providers who accept vouchers, and it may be a more efficient arrangement for providing supportive services. Initially, HUD limited the number of project-based vouchers to 50% of a PHA's total VASH allocation, but on September 15, 2011, HUD released a notice removing the 50% limit.[149] However, PHAs must still adhere to the requirements that the funding allocated for project-based vouchers does not exceed 20% of the PHA's tenant-based voucher budget, and that the local VA medical center must agree to the plan. If a veteran lives in a unit where HUD-VASH vouchers have been project based and wants to move, the PHA must provide the tenant with a Section 8 voucher or other tenant-based assistance.

On the same day that the third FY2010 voucher funding announcement was made, HUD released a notice of available funding for project-based HUD-VASH vouchers from the remaining FY2010 appropriation.[150] Funding for these project-based vouchers was awarded competitively, and any PHA that received an allocation of HUD-VASH vouchers in FY2008, FY2009, or FY2010 was eligible to apply. On June 13, 2011, HUD announced the award of 676 vouchers to PHAs in 18 states.[151] Another three PHAs that had applied for vouchers from the FY2010 appropriation received 99 vouchers funded through the FY2011 allocation. The VA announced the award on September 19, 2011, stating that the award was made "to fund additional applications that received high scores through HUD and VA's review process."[152]

Program Evaluations

The VA is collecting and evaluating data regarding the HUD-VASH vouchers that were funded beginning in FY2008, but has not yet released information.[153] However, some outcomes are available regarding participants who received vouchers in the early stages of the program. Long-term evaluations of the HUD-VASH program have shown both improved housing and improved substance abuse outcomes among veterans who received the vouchers over those who did not.[154]

Veterans who received vouchers experienced fewer days of homelessness and more days housed than veterans who received intensive case management assistance or standard care through VA homeless programs alone.[155] Analysis also found that veterans with HUD-VASH vouchers had fewer days of alcohol use, fewer days on which they drank to intoxication, and fewer days of drug use.[156] HUD-VASH veterans were also found to have spent fewer days in institutions.[157] Over the long term, veterans who received vouchers had a lower risk of returning to homelessness than those who received intensive case management or standard assistance.[158] Factors that increased the risk of returning to homelessness were alcohol or drug dependence and a diagnosis of PTSD.[159] Lower risk was found among those with psychiatric problems, possibly due to supportive services to assist those individuals with their housing.[160]

Demonstration Program to Prevent Homelessness among Veterans

As part of the FY2009 Omnibus Appropriations Act (P.L. 111-8), Congress appropriated $10 million through the HUD Homeless Assistance Grants account to be used for a pilot program to prevent homelessness among veterans. The appropriation law required that the program be operated in a limited number of sites, at least three of which were to have a large number of individuals transitioning from military to civilian life, and at least four of which were to be in rural areas. In July 2010, HUD issued a notice of implementation of the new demonstration program.[161] HUD, in consultation with the VA and DOL, selected five geographic areas in which local Continuums of Care (CoCs) will assign a grantee to carry out the prevention program. The areas were chosen based on the number of homeless veterans reported by the local CoC and VA Medical Center, the number of Operation Iraqi Freedom and Operation Enduring Freedom veterans accessing VA health care, the presence and diversity of military sites in the area (e.g., representation of different branches of the military, National Guard, and Reserves), availability of VA health care, type of geographic area (urban versus rural), and the community's capacity to administer the prevention program. The five areas and corresponding military bases selected are (1) San Diego, CA (Camp Pendleton); (2) Killeen, TX (Fort Hood); (3) Watertown, NY (Fort Drum); (4) Tacoma, WA (Joint Base Lewis-McChord); and (5) Tampa, FL (MacDill Air Force Base). The prevention program is to operate much like the Homelessness Prevention and Rapid Re-Housing Program that was created as part of the American Recovery and Reinvestment Act (P.L. 111-5). Funds may be used for short-term rental assistance (up to three months) or medium-term rental assistance (4-18 months), for up to six months of rental arrears, for security or utility deposits, utility payments, and help with moving expenses.[162] Recipients may also use funds for supportive services that help veterans and their families find and maintain housing such as case management, housing search and placement, credit repair, child care, and transportation.[163] To be eligible, veterans and their families must meet the following criteria:[164]

- have income at or below 50% of the area median income;
- be experiencing short-term homelessness or be at risk of losing housing;
- lack the resources or support networks to obtain housing or remain housed; and
- be experiencing instability as evidenced by one of the following: (1) living on the street or in shelter for less than 90 days, (2) being at least one month behind in rent, (3) facing eviction within two weeks, (4) being discharged from an institution, (5) living in condemned housing, (6) being behind on utility payments by at least a month, (7)

paying greater than 50% of income for housing, or (8) facing a sudden and significant loss of income.

The Department of Labor

The Department of Labor (DOL) contains an office specifically dedicated to the employment needs of veterans, the office of Veterans' Employment and Training Service (VETS). In addition to its program for homeless veterans— the Homeless Veterans Reintegration Program (HVRP)— VETS funds employment training programs for all veterans. These include the Veterans Workforce Investment Program and the Transition Assistance Program.

Homeless Veterans Reintegration Program

Established in 1987 as part of the McKinney-Vento Homeless Assistance Act (P.L. 100-77), the HVRP was authorized most recently through FY2012 as part of the Veterans Health Care Facilities Capital Improvement Act of 2011 (P.L. 112-37), which was signed into law on October 5, 2011. In 2010, the Veterans' Benefits Act of 2010 (P.L. 111-275) created a separate HVRP for women veterans and veterans with children. The new program, which includes child care among its services, is authorized from FY2011 through FY2015 at $1 million per year. The HVRP program has two goals. The first is to assist veterans in achieving meaningful employment, and the second is to assist in the development of a service delivery system to address the problems facing homeless veterans. Eligible grantee organizations are state and local Workforce Investment Boards, local public agencies, and both for- and non-profit organizations.[165] Grantees receive funding for one year, with the possibility for two additional years of funding contingent on performance and fund availability.[166] The DOL awards grants separately for urban and non-urban areas. HVRP grantee organizations provide services that include outreach, assistance in drafting a resume and preparing for interviews, job search assistance, subsidized trial employment, job training, and follow-up assistance after placement. Recipients of HVRP grants also provide supportive services not directly related to employment such as transportation, provision of assistance in finding housing, and referral for mental health treatment or substance abuse counseling. HVRP grantees often employ formerly homeless veterans to provide outreach to homeless veterans and to counsel them as they search for employment and stability. In fact, from the inception of the HVRP, it has been required that at least one employee of grantee organizations be a veteran who has experienced homelessness.[167] In program year (PY) 2007 (from July 1, 2007, through June 30, 2008), HVRP grantees were expected to serve a total of 13,446 homeless veterans, of whom an estimated 9,061, or 67%, were expected to be placed in employment.[168] In 2007, DOL predicted that 64.5% of veterans who were placed in employment would maintain employment for six months.[169] The previous year, 64% of veterans maintained employment for at least six months.

Stand Downs for Homeless Veterans

A battlefield stand down is the process in which troops are removed from danger and taken to a safe area to rest, eat, clean up, receive medical care, and generally recover from the stress and chaos of battle. Stand Downs for Homeless Veterans are modeled on the battlefield stand down and are local events, staged annually in many cities across the country, in which local Veterans Service Organizations, businesses, government entities, and other social service organizations come together for up to three days to provide similar services for homeless veterans. Items and services provided at stand downs include food, clothing, showers, haircuts, medical exams, dental care, immunizations, and, in some locations where stand downs take place for more than one day, shelter. Another important facet of stand downs, according to the National Coalition for Homeless Veterans, is the camaraderie that occurs when veterans spend time among other veterans. Although stand downs are largely supported through donations of funds, goods, and volunteer time, the DOL VETS office may award both HVRP grant recipient organizations or other organizations that would be eligible up to $10,000 to fund stand downs.[170]

Incarcerated Veterans Transition Program

The Homeless Veterans Comprehensive Assistance Act of 2001 (P.L. 107-95) instituted a demonstration program to provide job training and placement services to veterans leaving prison.[171] The program expired on January 24, 2006, but was extended by Congress through FY2012 as part of the Veterans' Mental Health and Other Care Improvements Act of 2008 (P.L. 110-387). The new law removed the program's demonstration status, expanded the number of sites able to provide services to 12, and changed the name slightly to "Referral and Counseling Services: Veterans at Risk of Homelessness Who Are Transitioning from Certain Institutions." Both the FY2010 and FY2011 Department of Labor budget documents state that of the funds requested for HVRP, up to $4 million would be used for this program.[172] On May 5, 2010, DOL published a solicitation for grant applications that was expected to fund at least 12 grants.[173] While in its demonstration phase, the program awarded $1.45 million in initial grants to seven recipients. DOL extended these seven grants through March 2006 with funding of $1.6 million, and then again for an additional 15 months, though June 30, 2007, with $2 million in funding.[174] The Department of Labor reported that these grant recipients enrolled 2,191 veterans in the transition program in FY2004 through FY2006 and that of these enrollees, 1,104, or 54%, entered employment.[175] The average wage for those veterans entering employment was $10.00 per hour.

FUNDING FOR HOMELESS VETERANS PROGRAMS

Table 6, below, shows historical funding levels for six programs that target services to homeless veterans. Following Table 6, Table 7 shows funding for housing provided through the HUD-VA collaboration known as HUD-VASH. HUD has funded Section 8 vouchers for homeless veterans since FY1992, but after the initial appropriation for the vouchers, HUD does not separately report the amount of funds necessary to provide rental assistance for each of the vouchers in subsequent years. Unlike programs included in Table 6, then, it is not possible to provide annual budget authority or obligations for HUD-VASH. Table 7 contains information regarding the initial budget authority needed to support the vouchers in the first year of appropriations.

ISSUES REGARDING VETERANS AND HOMELESSNESS

The VA Plan to End Veteran Homelessness

On November 3, 2009, the VA announced a plan to end homelessness among veterans within five years.[176] The VA outlined six areas of focus for the new plan in its FY2011 budget justifications: (1) outreach and education, (2) treatment, (3) prevention, (4) housing and supportive services, (5) employment and benefits, and (6) community partnerships.[177] In both the FY2011 and FY2012 budget documents, the VA laid out program expansions and implementation of new programs to address homelessness:

- In FY2012, the VA planned to expand some of the existing homeless programs discussed in this report. Specifically, the Grant and Per Diem Program would serve 20,000 veterans (in FY2008, the program discharged 15,511 veterans), the Domiciliary Care for Homeless Veterans program planned to open five new 40-bed facilities in FY2012, and the HUD-VASH program was to receive (and did receive) additional vouchers.
- The VA-HUD pilot to prevent veteran homelessness and the VA program of supportive services for very low-income veteran families have both gotten underway, with grants awarded to service providers. The VA expects to serve 1,900 veterans between 2011 and 2014 in the prevention pilot and 19,000 veterans in the SSVF program.
- The VA established a National Homeless Registry to keep records of veterans served in homeless-specific programs and measure outcomes achieved. The VA also established a National Call Center for homeless veterans that expects to serve 15,500 veterans in 2012.

During the last several years, estimates of homeless veterans have fallen. VA estimates of the number of veterans who were homeless on a given day fell from 154,000 in FY2007 to 131,000 in FY2008, and then to 107,000 in FY2009. The Veterans Supplement to HUD's Annual Homeless Assessment Report estimated that in 2011 the number had fallen to about 67,000, a nearly 9,000-person reduction from the previous year's estimate. (For more information, see the section of this report entitled "Estimates of the Number of Homeless Veterans.")

Table 6. Funding for Selected Homeless Veterans Programs, FY1988-FY2012 (dollars in thousands)

Fiscal Year	Obligations (VA Programs)					Budget Authority (DOL Program)
	Health Care for Homeless Veterans[a]	Domiciliary Care for Homeless Veterans	Compensated Work Therapy/ Therapeutic Residence	Grant and Per Diem Program	HUD-VA Supported Housing (Supportive Services)[b]	Homeless Veterans Reintegration Program
1988	12,932	15,000[c]	NA	NA	NA	1,915
1989	13,252	10,367	NA	NA	NA	1,877
1990	15,000	15,000	NA	NA	NA	1,920

Table 6. (Continued)

Fiscal Year	Obligations (VA Programs)					Budget Authority (DOL Program)
	Health Care for Homeless Veterans[a]	Domiciliary Care for Homeless Veterans	Compensated Work Therapy/ Therapeutic Residence	Grant and Per Diem Program	HUD-VA Supported Housing (Supportive Services)[b]	Homeless Veterans Reintegration Program
1991	15,461[d]	15,750	—[d]	NA	NA	2,018
1992	16,500[d]	16,500	—[d]	NA	2,300	1,366
1993	22,150	22,300	400	NA	2,000	5,055
1994	24,513	27,140	3,051	8,000	3,235	5,055
1995	38,585[c]	38,948	3,387	—[c]	4,270	107[f]
1996	38,433[c]	41,117	3,886	—[c]	4,829	0
1997	38,063[c]	37,214	3,628	—[c]	4,958	0
1998	36,407	38,489	8,612	5,886	5,084	3,000
1999	32,421	39,955	4,092	20,000	5,223	3,000
2000	38,381	34,434	8,068	19,640	5,137	9,636
2001	58,602	34,576	8,144	31,100	5,219	17,500
2002	54,135	45,443	8,028	22,431	4,729	18,250
2003	45,188	49,213	8,371	43,388	4,603	18,131
2004	42,905	51,829	10,240	62,965	3,375	18,888
2005	40,357	57,555	10,004	62,180	3,243	20,832
2006	56,998	63,592	19,529	63,621	5,297	21,780
2007	71,925	77,633	21,514	81,187	7,487	21,809
2008	77,656	96,098	21,497	114,696	4,854	23,620
2009	80,219	115,373	22,206	128,073	26,601	26,330
2010	109,727	175,979	61,205	175,057	71,137	36,330
2011[g]	135,932	140,949	52,788	217,639	151,069	36,257[h]
2012	—	—	—	—	—	38,185[i]

Sources: Department of Veterans Affairs Budget Justifications, FY1989-FY2012, VA Office of Homeless Veterans Programs, and Department of Labor Budget Justifications FY1989-FY2012.

a. Health Care for Homeless Veterans was originally called the Homeless Chronically Mentally Ill veterans program. In 1992, the VA began to use the title "Health Care for Homeless Veterans."

b. This column contains only the funding allocated from the VA for supportive services and does not include the cost of providing housing.

c. Congress appropriated funds for the DCHV program for both FY1987 and FY1988 (P.L. 100-71), however, the VA obligated the entire amount in FY1988. See VA Budget Summary for FY1989, Volume 2, Medical Benefits, p. 6-10.

d. For FY1991 and FY1992, funds from the Homeless Chronically Mentally Ill veterans program as well as substance abuse enhancement funds were used for the Compensated Work Therapy/Therapeutic Residence program.

e. For FY1995 through FY1997, Grant and Per Diem funds were obligated with funds for the Health Care for Homeless Veterans program. VA budget documents do not provide a separate breakdown of Grant and Per Diem Obligations.

f. Congress appropriated $5.011 million for HVRP in P.L. 103-333. However, a subsequent rescission in P.L. 104-19 reduced the amount.

g. The obligation amounts for FY2011 are estimates.

h. The FY2011 Department of Defense and Full-Year Continuing Appropriations Act (P.L. 112-10) imposed an across-the-board rescission of 0.2% on all discretionary accounts. The level for HVRP reflects this rescission.

i. The FY2012 appropriation for the Departments of Labor, HHS, and Education contained an across-the-board rescission of 0.189% on all discretionary accounts. The level for HVRP reflects this rescission.

During this same time period, the need for permanent housing, as reported by homeless veterans and those who provide services, has also declined. The VA's annual CHALENG report surveys homeless veterans, as well as government and community service providers, about the most pressing unmet needs among homeless veterans. Through FY2006, the highest priority unmet need according to all respondents in the CHALENG reports was long-term permanent housing.[178] However, in the FY2007 report, permanent housing was the second-highest unmet need, behind child care.[179] In FY2008 and FY2009, it fell to the fourth-highest unmet need,[180] and in FY2010, long-term housing was the ninth in the list of unmet needs for veterans.[181]

One of the reasons that estimates of homeless veterans are declining and that the highest unmet need is no longer housing could be an increasing emphasis on permanent supportive housing for veterans. The permanent supportive housing model promotes stability by ensuring that residents receive services tailored to their particular needs, including health care, counseling, employment assistance, help with financial matters, and assistance with other daily activities that might present challenges to a formerly homeless individual.

Historically, homeless programs targeted to veterans did not provide permanent supportive housing (although veterans were eligible for housing through HUD's homeless programs). Instead, programs such as Grant and Per Diem offered transitional housing to help veterans become stable, find employment, and eventually transition to permanent housing. However, after leaving transitional housing, veterans competed with other needy groups—

including elderly residents, persons with disabilities, and families with young children—for government assisted housing.[182] With the advent of HUD-VASH (discussed earlier in this report), thousands of units of permanent supportive housing funded through the federal government have been targeted to homeless veterans for the last five fiscal years. Congress has appropriated $350 million for the program, an amount sufficient to fund more than 40,000 vouchers for one year.[183] The additional Section 8 vouchers, as well as increased funding through VA programs interventions (see **Table 6**), could be making a difference in the number of veterans experiencing homelessness.

Table 7. Funding for HUD-VASH

Fiscal Year	Public Law	Amount Provided (dollars in millions)	Tenant-Based Vouchers Supported	Project-Based Vouchers Supported	Number of Years Vouchers Supported with Amount Provided
1992	NA[a]	17.9[b]	750	—	5
1993	NA[a]	19.1[c]	750	—	5
1994	NA[a]	18.4[d]	700	—	5
2008	P.L. 110-161	75.0	10,150[e]	—	1
2009	P.L. 111-8	75.0	10,290[e]	—	1
2010	P.L. 111-117	75.0	9,510[e]	676[f]	1
2011	P.L. 112-10	50.0	6,815[g]	99[h]	1
2012	P.L. 112-55	75.0	—	—	1
Total		**405.4**	**38,965[i]**	**775**	

Source: Sources for each voucher distribution are noted in the table notes, below.

a. Funding for FY1992 through FY1994 was set aside from Section 8 tenant-based appropriations.

b. The FY1992 announcement of the amount set aside and number of vouchers available was made in the *Federal Register*. See U.S. Department of Housing and Urban Development, "Invitation for FY1992 Section 8 Rental Voucher Set-Aside for Homeless Veterans with Severe Psychiatric or Substance Abuse Disorders," 57 *Federal Register* no. 55, pp. 9955-9968, March 20, 1992.

c. The announcement of the availability of funding and amount of vouchers to be funded in 1993 was made in U.S. Department of Housing and Urban Development, "Notice of Funding Availability (NOFA) for Fiscal Year 1993, for the Section 8 Set Aside for Homeless Veterans With Severe Psychiatric or Substance Abuse Disorders," 58 *Federal Register* no. 188, pp. 51191-51206, September 30, 1993.

d. The announcement of 1994 vouchers was made in U.S. Department of Housing and Urban Development, "Funding Availability (NOFA) for the Section 8 Set-Aside for Homeless Veterans with Severe Psychiatric or Substance Abuse Disorders," 59 *Federal Register* no. 134, pp. 36007-36015, July 14, 1994.

e. For a list of how the FY2008 through FY2010 tenant-based vouchers were allocated to local housing authorities, see http://www.hud.gov/offices/pih/programs/hcv/vash/docs/vash-awards.xls.

f. The list of project-based vouchers for FY2010 is available at http://portal.hud.gov/hudportal/documents/huddoc?id=HUD-VASHPBVFY2010AWARDEES.PDF. See also, U.S. Department of Housing and Urban Development, "HUD, VA to Provide Permanent Housing, Case Management to Nearly 700 Homeless Veterans Across the U.S.," press release, June 13, 2011, http://portal.hud.gov/hudportal/HUD?src=/press/press_releases_media_advisories/2011/HUDNo.11-118.

g. A list showing how FY2011 tenant-based vouchers were distributed is available at http://portal.hud.gov/hudportal/documents/huddoc?id=HUD-VASH2011CHART.PDF. See also, U.S. Department of Housing and Urban Development, "HUD, VA to Provide Permanent Housing and Support to Thousands of Homeless Veterans," press release, July 14, 2011, http://portal.hud.gov/hudportal/HUD?src=/press/press_releases_media_advisories/2011/HUDNo.11-150.

h. See Department of Veterans Affairs, "HUD, VA to Provide Permanent Housing, Case Management to Nearly 100 Homeless Veterans," press release, September 19, 2011, http://www.va.gov/opa/pressrel/pressrelease.cfm?id=2173.

i. Vouchers that were funded in FY1992-FY1994 may not have been provided to homeless veterans upon turnover. As a result, not all tenant-based vouchers in the total are necessarily still being used by homeless veterans.

Veterans of the Wars in Iraq and Afghanistan

As veterans return from Operation Iraqi Freedom (OIF) and Operation Enduring Freedom (OEF), just as veterans before them, they face risks that could lead to homelessness. The VA reported that in FY2009, it assessed almost 2,300 veterans who served in the OEF/OIF theaters of operations for participation in its Health Care for Homeless Veterans Program.[184] Approximately 1.40 million OEF/OIF troops have been separated from active duty and become eligible for VA health benefits since 2003.[185] If the experiences of the Vietnam War are any indication, the risk of becoming homeless continues for many years after service. One study found that after the Vietnam War, 76% of Vietnam era combat troops and 50% of non-combat troops who eventually became homeless reported that at least 10 years passed between the time they left military service and when they became homeless.[186]

A number of studies have examined the mental health status of troops returning from Iraq and Afghanistan. According to one study of troops returning from Iraq published in the New England Journal of Medicine, between 15% and 17% screened positive for depression, generalized anxiety, and PTSD.[187] Another study, conducted by the RAND Corporation, found that, of veterans surveyed, 14% reported screening positive for PTSD and 14% for major depression.[188] Veterans returning from Iraq also appear to be seeking out mental health services at higher rates than veterans returning from other conflicts.[189] Research has also found that the length and number of deployments of troops in Iraq result in greater risk of mental health problems.[190] Access to VA health services could be a critical component of reintegration into the community for some veterans, and there is concern that returning veterans might not be aware of available VA health programs and services.[191]

The VA has multiple means of reaching out to injured veterans and veterans currently receiving treatment through the Department of Defense (DOD) to ensure that they know about VA health services and to help them make the transition from DOD to VA services.[192] However, for some veterans, health issues, particularly mental health issues, may arise later. A study of Iraq soldiers returning from deployment found that a higher percentage of soldiers reported mental health concerns six months after returning than immediately after returning.[193]

Women Veterans

The number and percentage of women enlisted in the military have increased since previous wars. In FY2009, approximately 14.1% of enlisted troops in the active components of the military (Army, Navy, Air Force, and Marines) were female, up from approximately 3.3% in FY1974 and 10.9% in FY1990.[194] The number of women veterans can be expected to grow commensurately. According to the VA, there were approximately 1.2 million female veterans in 1990 (4% of the veteran population) and 1.6 million in 2000 (6%).[195] In 2010, approximately 1.8 million veterans were women.[196] The VA predicted that there would be 1.9 million female veterans (10% of the veteran population) in 2020. At the same time, the number of male veterans is expected to decline.[197]

Women veterans face challenges that could contribute to their risks of homelessness. A study of women veterans in the Los Angeles area compared homeless women veterans to women veterans who were housed and found that the characteristics most associated with homelessness were unemployment, having a disability, and being unmarried.[198] Additional factors associated with homelessness were screening positive for PTSD, experiencing military sexual trauma, suffering from an anxiety disorder, and having fair or poor health.

Experts have found that female veterans report incidents of sexual assault that exceed rates reported in the general population.[199] A study of all returning OEF/OIF veterans who used VA mental and/or primary health care found that 15.1% of female veterans reported experiencing sexual assault or harassment while in the military (referred to by the VA as military sexual trauma).[200] Veterans who had experienced military sexual trauma were more likely than other veterans to have been diagnosed with a mental health condition, including depressive disorders, PTSD, anxiety disorders, alcohol and substance use disorders, and adjustment disorders.[201] In particular, the relationship between military sexual trauma and PTSD among women was stronger than it was for men.[202] According to another study released in 2004, the percentage of all female veterans seeking medical care through the VA (not just those returning from Iraq or Afghanistan) who reported that they have experienced sexual assault ranged between 23% and 29%.[203] These factors can increase the difficulty with which women veterans readjust to civilian life, and could be risk factors for homelessness (see earlier discussion in this report).

Women veterans are estimated to make up a relatively small, but growing, proportion of the homeless veteran population. According to the 2010 Veterans Supplement to the Annual Homeless Assessment Report, homeless women veterans represented 8% of veterans living in shelter.[204] As a result, programs serving homeless veterans may not have adequate facilities for female veterans at risk of homelessness, particularly transitional housing for women and women with children. Currently, six Grant and Per Diem programs funded through the Special Needs Grant target women veterans,[205] and in FY2009, 4.4% of individuals placed in Grant and Per Diem programs were women[206] while 4.9% of veterans served in the Domiciliary Care for Homeless Veterans program in FY2009 were women.[207] The program that serves the highest percentage of female veterans is HUD-VASH; approximately 11% of veterans who have received vouchers are women.[208]

The need for assistance among younger women veterans, in particular, appears to be increasing. A report released by the VA about the risk and prevalence of homelessness among veterans noted the increased risk of homelessness among young, female veterans, and that intervention upon return from service and during the transition to civilian life could benefit this group.[209] It is also noteworthy that child care was the highest unmet need reported by homeless veterans and service providers as part of the last four VA CHALENG reports.

In the 110th Congress, the Veterans' Mental Health and Other Care Improvements Act of 2008 (110-387) added a provision to the statute governing the Domiciliary Care for Homeless Veterans program requiring the Secretary to "take appropriate actions to ensure that the domiciliary care programs of the Department are adequate, with respect to capacity and with respect to safety, to meet the needs of veterans who are women." In the 111th Congress, the Veterans' Benefits Act of 2010 (P.L. 111-275), signed into law on October 13, 2010, created an HVRP grant program specifically targeted to serve women veterans and veterans with children. The new program, like HVRP, will provide job training, counseling, and job placement services, but will also provide child care for participants. The program is authorized from FY2011 through FY2015 at $1 million per year.

End Notes

[1] Peter H. Rossi, *Down and Out in America: The Origins of Homelessness* (Chicago: The University of Chicago Press, 1989), 181-194, 41. See, also, Martha Burt, *Over the Edge: The Growth of Homelessness in the 1980s* (New York: Russell Sage Foundation, 1992), 31-126.

[2] *Down and Out in America*, p. 34; *Over the Edge*, p. 123.

[3] See Randall Kuhn and Dennis P. Culhane, "Applying Cluster Analysis to Test a Typology of Homelessness by Pattern of Shelter Utilization: Results from the Analysis of Administrative Data," *American Journal of Community Psychology* 26, no. 2 (April 1998): 210-212.

[4] Martha R. Burt, Laudan Y. Aron et al., *Homelessness: Programs and the People They Serve, Technical Report*, Urban Institute, December 1999, p. 11-1, available at http://www.huduser.org/Publications/pdf/home_tech/tchap-11.pdf. Of homeless male veterans surveyed, 32% reported being homeless for 13 or more months, versus 17% of nonveteran homeless men.

[5] Marjorie J. Robertson, "Homeless Veterans, An Emerging Problem?" in *The Homeless in Contemporary Society*, ed. Richard J. Bingham, Roy E. Green, and Sammis B. White (Newbury Park, CA: Sage Publications, 1987), 66.

[6] Ibid., pp. 64-65.

[7] The United States Code defines the term as "a veteran who is homeless" as defined by the McKinney-Vento Homeless Assistance Act. 38 U.S.C. §2002(1).

[8] 12 U.S.C. §101(2).

[9] The definition of "homeless veteran" is at 39 U.S.C. § 2002. The McKinney-Vento definition of homeless individual is codified at 42 U.S.C. §11302(a).

[10] For more information about the definition of homelessness and other HEARTH Act changes, see CRS Report RL33764, *The HUD Homeless Assistance Grants: Current Operation and HEARTH Act Changes*, by Libby Perl.

[11] U.S. Department of Housing and Urban Development, *Guidance for Counting Veterans During 2011 Point-in-Time Counts of Homeless People*, p. 2, http://www.hudhre.info/documents/2011PITVetGuidance.pdf.

[12] Continuums of Care are typically formed by cities, counties, or combinations of both. Representatives from local government agencies and service provider organizations serve on CoC boards, which conduct the business of the CoC.

[13] For results of the most recent count in which all CoCs participated and for which results are available (2009), see http://www.hudhre.info/CoC_Reports/2009_pops_sub_FULL.pdf. The 2011 count has taken place, but results are not yet available.

[14] U.S. Department of Housing and Urban Development, *The 2010 Annual Homeless Assessment Report to Congress*, June 2011, p. 5, http://www.hudhre.info/documents/2010Homeless AssessmentReport.pdf (hereinafter, *Sixth AHAR*).

[15] *Guidance for Counting Veterans During 2011 Point-in-Time Counts of Homeless People*, p. 2.

[16] U.S. Department of Housing and Urban Development and U.S. Department of Veterans Affairs, *Veteran Homelessness: A Supplemental Report to the 2009 Annual Homeless Assessment Report to Congress*, January 2011, http://www.hudhre.info/documents/2009 AHARVeteransReport.pdf.

[17] Ibid., p. 5.

[18] Ibid., Appendix A.

[19] Ibid., p. 5.

[20] Ibid.

[21] Ibid., Appendix A.

[22] Ibid., p. 6.

[23] U.S. Department of Housing and Urban Development and U.S. Department of Veterans Affairs, *Veteran Homelessness: A Supplemental Report to the 2010 Annual Homeless Assessment Report to Congress*, October 2011, http://www.hudhre.info/documents/2010 AHARVeteransReport.pdf (hereinafter *FY2010 AHAR Veterans Supplement*).

[24] Ibid., p. 3.

[25] Ibid., p. 4.

[26] Ibid., p. 3.

[27] Ibid., Appendix A.

[28] Ibid., p. 4.

[29] U.S. Department of Housing and Urban Development, *The 2011 Point-in-Time Estimates of Homelessness: Supplement to the Annual Homeless Assessment Report*, December 2011, p. 6, http://www.hudhre.info/documents/PIT-HIC_SupplementalAHARReport.pdf.

[30] Congress required the VA to issue the report as part of the Veterans Benefits Improvement Act of 1994, P.L. 103-446 (38 U.S.C. §2065).

[31] *The Seventeenth Annual Progress Report on P.L. 105-114: Services for Homeless Veterans Assessment and Coordination*, U.S. Department of Veterans Affairs, July 5, 2011, p. 23, http://www.va.gov/HOMELESS/docs/chaleng/CHALENG_Report_Seventeenth_Annual.pd f (hereinafter, *Seventeenth Annual CHALENG Report*).

[32] John H. Kuhn and John Nakashima, *The Sixteenth Annual Progress Report on P.L. 105-114: Services for Homeless Veterans Assessment and Coordination*, U.S. Department of Veterans Affairs, March 17, 2010, p. 23, http://www1.va.gov/HOMELESS/docs/chaleng/ chaleng_sixteenth_annual_report.pdf (hereinafter, *Sixteenth Annual CHALENG Report*).

[33] Government Accountability Office, *Homeless Veterans Programs: Improved Communications and Follow-up Could Further Enhance the Grant and Per Diem Program*, GAO-06-859, September 2006, p. 13, http://www.gao.gov/new.items/d06859.pdf.

[34] *FY2010 AHAR Veterans Supplement*, pp. 7-11.

[35] According to data from the National Center for Veteran Analysis and Statistics, African Americans made up 11.6% of the veteran population in 2009. See http://www1.va.gov/ VETDATA/docs/Demographics/5l.xls.

[36] In 2009, veterans who served between the Vietnam and Gulf War eras comprised 14.8% of veterans. See http://www.va.gov/VETDATA/docs/Demographics/2l.xls.

[37] Bureau of Labor Statistics, *Employment Situation of Veterans 2009*, March 12, 2010, http:// www.bls.gov/news.release/archives/vet_03122010.htm.

[38] The marriage rates of veterans generally is from U.S. Department of Veterans Affairs, *Profile of Veterans 2009*, January 2011, p. 7, http://www.va.gov/vetdata/docs/SpecialReports/ Profile_of_Veterans_2009_FINAL.pdf.

[39] Robert Rosenheck, Catherine A. Leda, and Linda K. Frisman, et al., "Homeless Veterans," in *Homelessness in America*, ed. Jim Baumohl (Phoenix: The Oryx Press, 1996), pp. 104-105 (hereinafter "Homeless Veterans").

[40] Ibid., p. 105.

[41] Richard Tessler, Robert Rosenheck, and Gail Gamache, "Comparison of Homeless Veterans with Other Homeless Men in a Large Clinical Outreach Program," *Psychiatric Quarterly* 73, no. 2 (Summer 2002): 113-114.

[42] Veterans averaged 12.43 years of education completed, versus 11.21 for nonveterans.

[43] Family instability is measured by factors that include parental separation or divorce and time spent in foster care.

[44] Conduct disorder is measured by factors such as school suspensions, expulsions, drinking, using drugs, stealing, and fighting.

[45] Gail Gamache, Robert Rosenheck, and Richard Tessler, "Overrepresentation of Women Veterans Among Homeless Women," *American Journal of Public Health* 93, no. 7 (July 2003): 1133-1134 (hereinafter "Overrepresentation of Women Veterans Among Homeless Women").

[46] Martha R. Burt, Laudan Y. Aron, et al., *Homelessness: Programs and the People They Serve: Findings of the National Survey of Homeless Assistance Providers and Clients, Technical Report*, December 1999, available at http://www.huduser.org/publications/homeless/homeless_tech.html.

[47] Martha R. Burt and Barbara E. Cohen, *America's Homeless: Numbers, Characteristics, and Programs that Serve Them* (Washington, DC: The Urban Institute Press, July 1989).

[48] See Jamison Fargo, Stephen Metraux, and Thomas Byrne, et al., "Prevalence and Risk of Homelessness Among U.S. Veterans," *Preventing Chronic Disease*, vol. 9 (January 26, 2012), http://www.cdc.gov/pcd/issues/2012/11_0112.htm(hereinafter Prevalence and Risk of Homelessness Among U.S. Veterans). In addition, preliminary information had been made available on the National Center on Homelessness Among Veterans website, http://www.va.gov/HOMELESS/docs/Center/Prevalence_Final.pdf.

[49] See Gail Gamache, Robert Rosenheck, and Richard Tessler, "The Proportion of Veterans Among Homeless Men: A Decade Later," *Social Psychiatry and Psychiatric Epidemiology* 36, no. 10 (October 2001): 481 (hereinafter, "The Proportion of Homeless Veterans Among Men: A Decade Later"). "Overrepresentation of Women Veterans Among Homeless Women," p. 1134; and Prevalence and Risk of Homelessness Among U.S. Veterans, Table 2.

[50] Generally, the Vietnam era is defined as the period from 1964 to 1975. 38 U.S.C. §101(29)(B).

[51] Alvin S. Mares and Robert A. Rosenheck, "Perceived Relationship Between Military Service and Homelessness Among Homeless Veterans with Mental Illness," *The Journal of Nervous and Mental Disease* 192, no. 10 (October 2004): 715.

[52] See Robert Rosenheck, Linda Frisman, and An-Me Chung, "The Proportion of Veterans Among Homeless Men," *American Journal of Public Health* 84, no. 3 (March 1994): 466 (hereinafter, "The Proportion of Homeless Veterans Among Men"); "The Proportion of Veterans Among Homeless Men: A Decade Later," p. 481.

[53] "The Proportion of Homeless Veterans Among Men," p. 467.

[54] Ibid.

[55] "The Proportion of Homeless Veterans Among Men: A Decade Later," p. 483.

[56] Prevalence and Risk of Homelessness Among U.S. Veterans, Table 2.

[57] "Overrepresentation of Women Veterans Among Homeless Women," p. 1133.

[58] Ibid., p. 1134.

[59] Prevalence and Risk of Homelessness Among U.S. Veterans, Table 2.

[60] Ibid., Discussion section.

[61] The quote appeared in preliminary VA research using the 2009 HMIS data. See Jamison Fargo, Stephen Metraux, and Thomas Byrne, et al., *Prevalence and Risk of Homelessness Among U.S. Veterans: A Multisite Investigation*, U.S. Department of Veterans Affairs ,

August 2011, p. 24, http://www.va.gov/HOMELESS/docs/Center/ Prevalence_Final.pdf (hereinafter *Prevalence and Risk of Homelessness Among U.S. Veterans: A Multisite Investigation*).

[62] The NVVRS was undertaken at the direction of Congress as part of P.L. 98-160, the Veterans Health Care Amendments of 1983.

[63] Robert Rosenheck and Alan Fontana, "A Model of Homelessness Among Male Veterans of the Vietnam War Generation," *The American Journal of Psychiatry* 151, no. 3 (March 1994): 421-427 (hereinafter, "A Model of Homelessness Among Male Veterans of the Vietnam War Generation").

[64] See, for example, Alvin S. Mares and Robert Rosenheck, "Perceived Relationship Between Military Service and Homelessness Among Homeless Veterans With Mental Illness," *Journal of Nervous and Mental Disease* 192, no. 10 (October 2004): 715.

[65] Richard A. Kulka, John A. Fairbank, B. Kathleen Jordan, and Daniel S. Weiss, *Trauma and the Vietnam War Generation: Report of Findings from the National Vietnam Veterans Readjustment Study* (Levittown, PA: Brunner/Mazel, 1990), 142.

[66] The first category consisted of nine factors: year of birth, belonging to a racial or ethnic minority, childhood poverty, parental mental illness, experience of physical or sexual abuse prior to age 18, other trauma, treatment for mental illness before age 18, placement in foster care before age 16, and history of conduct disorder. The military category contained three factors: exposure to combat, participation in atrocities, and non-military trauma. The readjustment period consisted of two variables: accessibility to someone with whom to discuss personal matters and the availability of material and social support (together these two variables were termed low levels of social support). The final category contained four factors: Post Traumatic Stress Disorder (PTSD), psychiatric disorders not including PTSD, substance abuse, and unmarried status.

[67] "A Model of Homelessness Among Male Veterans of the Vietnam War Generation," p. 424.

[68] Ibid., p. 425.

[69] "A Model of Homelessness Among Male Veterans of the Vietnam War Generation," p. 425.

[70] Robert Rosenheck, Catherine A. Leda, Linda K. Frisman, Julie Lam, and An-Me Chung, "Homeless Veterans" in *Homelessness in America*, ed. Jim Baumohl (Phoenix, AZ: Oryx Press, 1996), 99 (hereinafter, "Homeless Veterans").

[71] Robert Rosenheck, Catherine Leda, and Peggy Gallup, "Combat Stress, Psychosocial Adjustment, and Service Use Among Homeless Vietnam Veterans," *Hospital and Community Psychiatry* 42, no. 2 (February 1992): 148.

[72] "Homeless Veterans," p. 98.

[73] "A Model of Homelessness Among Male Veterans of the Vietnam War Generation," p. 426.

[74] Ibid.

[75] Richard Tessler, Robert Rosenheck, and Gail Gamache, "Homeless Veterans of the All-Volunteer Force: A Social Selection Perspective," *Armed Forces & Society* 29, no. 4 (Summer 2003): 511 (hereinafter, "Homeless Veterans of the All-Volunteer Force: A Social Selection Perspective").

[76] Testimony of Robert Rosenheck, M.D., Director of Northeast Program Evaluation Center, Department of Veterans Affairs, Senate Committee on Veterans' Affairs, 103rd Cong., 2nd sess., February 23, 1994.

[77] "Homeless Veterans of the All-Volunteer Force: A Social Selection Perspective," p. 510.

[78] Senate Committee on Veterans Affairs, *Veterans' Administration FY1988 Budget, the Vet Center Program, and Homeless Veterans Issues*, 100th Cong., 1st sess., S.Hrg. 100-350, February 18 & 19, 1987, p. 2-6.

[79] For more information about the VHA, see CRS Report R41944, *Veterans' Medical Care: FY2012 Appropriations*, by Sidath Viranga Panangala.

[80] For more information about veterans benefits, see CRS Report RS22804, *Veterans' Benefits: Pension Benefit Programs*, by Christine Scott and Carol D. Davis and CRS Report

RL34626, *Veterans' Benefits: Benefits Available for Disabled Veterans*, by Christine Scott, Carol D. Davis, and Libby Perl.

[81] For more information about educational assistance, see CRS Report R40723, *Educational Assistance Programs Administered by the U.S. Department of Veterans Affairs*, by Cassandra Dortch.

[82] For more information about VA home loan guarantees, see CRS Report RS20533, *VA-Home Loan Guaranty Program: An Overview*, by Bruce E. Foote.

[83] For more information about the organization of the VA, see U.S. Department of Veterans Affairs, *2010 Organizational Briefing Book*, June 2010, http://www4.va.gov/ofcadmin/docs/vaorgbb.pdf.

[84] In 1992, the VA began to refer to the program by its new name. VA FY1994 Budget Summary, Volume 2, Medical Benefits, p. 2-63.

[85] Shortly after the HCHV program was enacted in P.L. 100-6, Congress passed another law (P.L. 100-322) that repealed the authority in P.L. 100-6 and established the HCHV program as a pilot program. The program was then made permanent in the Veterans Benefits Act of 1997 (P.L. 105-114). The HCHV program is now codified at 38 U.S.C. §§2031-2034.

[86] 38 U.S.C. §2031, §2034.

[87] Veterans Administration, Report to Congress of member agencies of the Interagency Council on Homelessness pursuant to Section 203(c)(1) of P.L. 100-77, October 15, 1987.

[88] Wesley J. Kasprow, Timothy Cuerdon, Diane DiLello, Leslie Cavallaro, and Nicole Harelik, *Healthcare for Homeless Veterans Programs: Twenty-Third Annual Report*, U.S. Department of Veterans Affairs Northeast Program Evaluation Center, March 25, 2010, Executive Summary, p. i (hereinafter, *Healthcare for Homeless Veterans Programs: Twenty-Third Annual Report*).

[89] The program was most recently authorized in the Veterans Health Care Facilities Capital Improvement Act of 2011 (P.L. 112-37).

[90] FY2004 VA Budget Justifications, p. 2-163.

[91] *Healthcare for Homeless Veterans Programs: Twenty-Third Annual Report*, pp. 121-122.

[92] Ibid., p. 23.

[93] Ibid., p. 26.

[94] Ibid., p. 144.

[95] Ibid., p. 123.

[96] Catherine Leda Seibyl, Sharon Medak, Linda Baldino, and Timonthy Cuerdon, *Twenty-First Progress Report on the Domiciliary Care for Homeless Veterans Program, FY2009*, U.S. Department of Veterans Affairs Northeast Program Evaluation Center, March 24, 2010, p. 2 (hereinafter, *Twenty-First Progress Report on the Domiciliary Care for Homeless Veterans Program*).

[97] Ibid., p. 7.

[98] Ibid., pp. 8-9.

[99] Ibid., p. 9.

[100] Senate Veterans Affairs Committee, report to accompany S. 2908, 94th Cong., 2nd sess., S.Rept. 94-1206, September9, 1976.

[101] The CWT program is codified at 38 U.S.C. §1718.

[102] 38 U.S.C. §1718(c).

[103] Sandra D. Resnick, Richard Kaczynski, Debbie Sieffert, et. al., *Thirteenth Progress Report on the Compensated Work Therapy (CWT) Program, Fiscal Year 2009*, Department of Veterans Affairs Northeast Program Evaluation Center, Table 29 (hereinafter, *Thirteenth Progress Report on the Compensated Work Therapy (CWT) Program*).

[104] The program was last authorized as part of the Veterans Health Care Facilities Capital Improvement Act of 2011 P.L. 112-37. See 38 U.S.C. §2031.

[105] The VA's authority to operate therapeutic housing is codified at 38 U.S.C. §2032.

[106] The provision for nonprofits was in P.L. 102-54, but was repealed by P.L. 105-114, §1720A(c)(1).

[107] Catherine Leda Seibyl, Sharon Medak, Linda Baldino, and Timothy Cuerdon, *Compensated Work Therapy/Transitional Residence (CWT/TR) Program Fiscal Year 2009*, Department of Veterans Affairs, Northeast Program Evaluation Center, June 2010, report summary.

[108] Ibid., Table 4.

[109] Ibid.

[110] *Thirteenth Progress Report on the Compensated Work Therapy (CWT) Program*, Table 5.

[111] Ibid., Table 6.

[112] Ibid.

[113] Ibid.

[114] The Grant and Per Diem program is codified at 38 U.S.C. §§2011-2013.

[115] U.S. Department of Veterans Affairs, *FY2012 Congressional Budget Justification, Volume II, Medical Programs and Information Technology*, p. 1H-12, http://www.va.gov/budget/docs/summary/Fy2012_Volume_II-Medical_Programs_Information_Technology.pdf.

[116] 38 U.S.C. §2011(c).

[117] 38 CFR §61.1.

[118] 38 CFR §61.33.

[119] U.S. Department of Veterans Affairs website, Frequently Asked Questions, accessed March 8, 2011, http://www.va.gov/HOMELESS/GPD_FAQ.asp.

[120] *2009 Annual Report of the Advisory Committee on Homeless Veterans*, July 1, 2009, p. 9, http://www1.va.gov/advisory/docs/ReportHomeless2009.pdf (hereinafter, *2009 Advisory Committee on Homeless Veterans Report*).

[121] *Healthcare for Homeless Veterans Programs: Twenty-Third Annual Report*, Table 5-1, p. 193.

[122] Ibid., p. 173.

[123] 38 C.F.R. §61.80(d) and §61.33(e).

[124] *Healthcare for Homeless Veterans Programs: Twenty-Third Annual Report*, Table 5-11, p. 231.

[125] Ibid., p. 174.

[126] Ibid., Table 5-13, p. 235.

[127] Ibid., Table 5-14, p. 239.

[128] U.S. Department of Veterans Affairs, "VA Launches New Prevention Initiative to Serve 22,000 Veteran Families at Risk of Homelessness," press release, July 26, 2011, http://www.va.gov/opa/pressrel/pressrelease.cfm?id=2139.

[129] U.S. Department of Veterans Affairs, "Fund Availability Under the Supportive Services for Veteran Families Program," 76 *Federal Register* 74850, December 1, 2011.

[130] 38 U.S.C. §§8161-8169.

[131] 38 U.S.C. §8162.

[132] Ibid.

[133] U.S. Department of Veterans Affairs, *FY2012 Congressional Budget Justification, Volume IV: Construction and the 10 Year Capital Plan*, Appendix E, http://www.va.gov/budget/docs/summary/Fy2012_Appendix-10_Year_Plan.pdf.

[134] Ibid., Appendix F.

[135] U.S. Department of Veterans Affairs, "VA to Expand Housing for Homeless Veterans and Their Families," press release, June 8, 2011, http://www.va.gov/opa/pressrel/pressrelease.cfm?id=2113.

[136] The program was most recently authorized in the Veterans Health Care Facilities Capital Improvement Act of 2011 (P.L. 112-37). The program is codified at 38 U.S.C. §2041.

[137] The first announcement of voucher availability was made in the *Federal Register*. See U.S. Department of Housing and Urban Development, "Invitation for FY1992 Section 8 Rental Voucher Set-Aside for Homeless Veterans with Severe Psychiatric or Substance Abuse Disorders," 57 *Federal Register* no. 55, p. 9955, March 20, 1992.

[138] U.S. Department of Housing and Urban Development, "Funding Availability (NOFA) for the Section 8 Set-Aside for Homeless Veterans with Severe Psychiatric or Substance Abuse Disorders," 59 *Federal Register* no. 134, p. 36015, July 14, 1994.

[139] *Healthcare for Homeless Veterans Programs: Twenty-Second Annual Report*, p. 279.

[140] 42 U.S.C. §1437f(o)(19).

[141] With the exception of those involving fair housing, nondiscrimination, labor standards, and the environment.

[142] U.S. Department of Housing and Urban Development, "Section 8 Housing Choice Vouchers: Implementation of the HUD-VA Supportive Housing Program," 73 *Federal Register* 25027, May 6, 2008.

[143] For a list of how the FY2008 and FY2009 vouchers were allocated to local housing authorities, see http://www.hud.gov/offices/pih/programs/hcv/vash/docs/vash-awards.xls.

[144] A table of the vouchers allocated to each housing authority is available at http://portal.hud.gov/portal/page/portal/HUD/documents/hud-vash2010round1.pdf.

[145] A table showing the allocation of the second round of vouchers is available at http://portal.hud.gov/portal/page/portal/HUD/documents/hudvash2010.pdf.

[146] The funding chart is available on HUD's website at http://portal.hud.gov/portal/page/portal/HUD/documents/hud-vashr3_fundingchart.pdf.

[147] U.S. Department of Housing and Urban Development, "HUD, VA to Provide Permanent Housing and Support to Thousands of Homeless Veterans," press release, July 14, 2011, http://portal.hud.gov/hudportal/HUD?src=/press/press_releases_media_advisories/2011/HUDNo.11-150.

[148] VA summary of HUD-VASH voucher performance provided to CRS.

[149] U.S. Department of Housing and Urban Development, Notice PIH 2011-50, *Project-Basing HUD-Veterans Affairs Supportive Housing Vouchers*, September 15, 2011, http://portal.hud.gov/hudportal/documents/huddoc?id=11-50pihn.doc.

[150] U.S. Department of Housing and Urban Development, Notice PIH 2010-40, *Set-Aside Funding Availability for Project-Basing HUD-Veterans Affairs Supportive Housing Vouchers*, September 28, 2010, http://portal.hud.gov/portal/page/portal/HUD/program_offices/administration/hudclips/notices/pih/files/10-40pihn.pdf.

[151] U.S. Department of Housing and Urban Development, "HUD, VA to Provide Permanent Housing, Case Management to Nearly 700 Homeless Veterans Across the U.S.," press release, June 13, 2011, http://portal.hud.gov/hudportal/HUD?src=/press/press_releases_media_advisories/2011/HUDNo.11-118.

[152] U.S. Department of Veterans Affairs, "HUD, VA to Provide Permanent Housing, Case Management to Nearly 100 Homeless Veterans," press release, September 19, 2011, http://www.va.gov/opa/pressrel/pressrelease.cfm?id=2173.

[153] *Healthcare for Homeless Veterans Programs: Twenty-Second Annual Report*, p. 277.

[154] Robert Rosenheck, Wesley Kasprow, Linda Frisman, and Wen Liu-Mares, "Cost-effectiveness of Supported Housing for Homeless Persons with Mental Illness," *Archives of General Psychiatry* 60 (September 2003): 940(hereinafter, "Cost-effectiveness of Supported Housing for Homeless Persons with Mental Illness"). An-Lin Cheng,Haiqun Lin, Wesley Kasprow, and Robert Rosenheck, "Impact of Supported Housing on Clinical Outcomes," *Journal of Nervous and Mental Disease* 195, no. 1 (January 2007): 83 (hereinafter, "Impact of Supported Housing on ClinicalOutcomes").

[155] "Cost-effectiveness of Supported Housing for Homeless Persons with Mental Illness," p. 945.

[156] "Impact of Supported Housing on Clinical Outcomes," p. 85.

[157] Ibid.

[158] Maria J. O'Connell, Wesley Kasprow, and Robert A. Rosenheck, "Rates and Risk Factors for Homelessness After Successful Housing in a Sample of Formerly Homeless Veterans," *Psychiatric Services*, vol. 59, no. 3 (March 2008), pp. 268-275.

[159] Ibid., p. 270.

[160] Ibid., p. 273.

[161] U.S. Department of Housing and Urban Development, *Notice of FY2009 Implementation of the Veterans Homelessness Prevention Demonstration Program*, July 14, 2010, http://www.hudhre.info/documents/VetsHomelessPreventionDemo.pdf.

[162] Ibid., pp. 9-11.

[163] Ibid., p. 11.

[164] Ibid., pp. 13-14.

[165] U.S. Department of Labor, Veterans' Employment and Training Service, Solicitation for Grant Applications, Urban and Non-Urban Homeless Veterans' Reintegration Program (HVRP) Grants For Program Year (PY) 2010, March 26, 2010, p. 21, http://www.dol.gov/vets/grants/2010/HVRP%20PY%202010%20SGA%20%28PDF%29.pdf.

[166] Ibid., p. 18.

[167] "Procedures for Preapplication for Funds; Stewart B. McKinney Homeless Assistance Act, FY1988" *Federal Register* vol. 53, no. 70, April 12, 1988, p. 12089.

[168] U.S. Department of Labor, Office of the Assistance Secretary for Veterans' Employment and Training, *FY2006 and FY2007 Annual Report to Congress*, May 21, 2008, p. 10,.

[169] U.S. Department of Labor, Office of Veterans' Employment and Training, *FY2008 VETS Annual Report to Congress*, p. 5, http://www.dol.gov/vets/media/FY2008_Annual_Report_To_Congress.pdf.

[170] U.S. Department of Labor, Veterans' Employment and Training Service, "FY2011 through FY2013 Stand Down Grant Requests," 76 *Federal Register* 13236-13239, March 10, 2011.

[171] 38 U.S.C. §2023.

[172] U.S. Department of Labor, *FY2010 Congressional Budget Justification*, Volume III, Veterans' Employment and Training Service, p. VETS-26, http://www.dol.gov/dol/budget/2010/PDF/CBJ-2010-V3-06.pdf; *FY2011 Congressional Budget Justification*, Volume III, Veterans' Employment and Training Service, p. VETS-37, http://www.dol.gov/dol/budget/2011/PDF/CBJ-2011-V3-05.pdf.

[173] The solicitation is available at http://www.dol.gov/vets/programs/ivtp/main.htm.

[174] *Vets Employment and Training Service FY2006 and FY2007 Annual Report to Congress*, p. 12.

[175] Ibid., 13.

[176] See U.S. Department of Veterans Affairs, "Secretary Shinseki Details Plan to End Homelessness for Veterans," press release, November 3, 2009, http://www1.va.gov/OPA/pressrel/pressrelease.cfm?id=1807.

[177] *FY2011 VA Budget Justifications*, p. 1K-11.

[178] *The Fifteenth Annual CHALENG Report*, p. 14.

[179] *The Fourteenth Annual CHALENG Report*, p. 8.

[180] *The Fifteenth Annual CHALENG Report*, p. 10, and *The Sixteenth Annual CHALENG Report*, p. 12.

[181] *Seventeenth Annual CHALENG Report*, p. 12.

[182] According to a 2007 GAO study, veteran households were underrepresented in HUD-assisted housing. GAO estimated that 11% of low-income veteran renter households received HUD rental assistance compared to 19% of low-income nonveteran renter households. Government Accountability Office, *Information on Low-Income Veterans' Housing Needs Conditions and Participation in HUD's Programs*, GAO-07-1012, August 17, 2007, p. 29, available at http://www.gao.gov/new.items/d071012.pdf.

[183] See the FY2008 Consolidated Appropriations Act (P.L. 110-161), the FY2009 Omnibus Appropriations Act (P.L. 111-8), the FY2010 Consolidated Appropriations Act (P.L. 111-117), the FY2011 Department of Defense and Full-Year Continuing Appropriations Act (P.L. 112-10), and the FY2012 Consolidated and Further Continuing Appropriations Act (P.L. 112-55).

[184] *Healthcare for Homeless Veterans Programs: Twenty-Third Annual Report*, p. 46.

[185] Since October 2003, DOD's Defense Manpower Data Center (DMDC) has periodically (every 60 days) sent VA an updated personnel roster of troops who participated in OEF and OIF, and who have separated from active duty and become eligible for VA benefits. The roster was originally prepared based on pay records of individuals. However, in more recent months it has been based on a combination of pay records and operational records provided

by each service branch. The current separation data are from FY2002 through December
2011. Note that the total includes veterans who died in-theater (5,584).

[186] See "Homeless Veterans," p. 105.

[187] Charles W. Hoge, Carl A. Castro, Stephen C. Messer, and Dennis McGurk, "Combat Duty in
Iraq and Afghanistan, Mental Health Problems, and Barriers to Care," *New England
Journal of Medicine* 351, no. 1 (July 1, 2004): Table 3.

[188] Terri Tanielian and Lisa H. Jaycox, eds., *Invisible Wounds of War: Psychological and
Cognitive Injuries, Their Consequences, and Services to Assist Recovery* (Santa Monica,
CA: RAND Corporation, 2008) 96.

[189] Charles W. Hoge, Jennifer L. Auchterlonie, and Charles S. Milliken, "Mental Health
Problems, Use of Mental Health Services, and Attrition from Military Service After
Returning from Deployment to Iraq or Afghanistan," *JAMA* 295, no. 9 (March 1, 2006):
1026, 1029.

[190] Office of the Surgeon Multi-National Force-Iraq and Office of the Surgeon General United
States Army Command, *Mental Health Advisory Team V*, February 14, 2008, pp. 42-43, 46-
47, available at http://www.armymedicine.army.mil/reports/mhat/mhat_v/MHAT_V_OIF
andOEF-Redacted.pdf.

[191] See, for example, Amy Fairweather, *Risk and Protective Factors for Homelessness Among
OIF/OEF Veterans*, Swords to Plowshares' Iraq Veteran Project, December 7, 2006, p. 6.

[192] For more information about transition services, see the National Resource Directory, http://
www.nationalresourcedirectory.gov/.

[193] Charles S. Milliken, Jennifer L. Auchterlonie, and Charles W. Hoge, "Longitudinal
Assessment of Mental Health Problems Among Active and Reserve Component Soldiers
Returning from the Iraq War," *JAMA* 298, no. 18(November 14, 2007): 2141, 2144.

[194] U.S. Department of Defense, Office of the Under Secretary of Defense, Personnel and
Readiness, *Population Representation in the Military Services, FY2010*, Appendix D, Table
D-13, http://prhome.defense.gov/MPP/ACCESSION%20POLICY/PopRep2010/appendixd/
d_13.html. Female enlistment reached its peak in FY2002 andFY2003 at 15.0%.

[195] Robert A. Klein, *Women Veterans: Past, Present, and Future*, U.S. Department of Veterans
Affairs, Office of the Actuary, updated September 2007, pp. 8-9, available at http://www1.
va.gov/vetdata/docs/Womenveterans_past_present_future_9-30-07a.pdf.

[196] U.S. Census Bureau, *2012 Statistical Abstract*, Table 521, http://www.census.gov/
compendia/statab/2012/tables/12s0520.pdf.

[197] *Women Veterans: Past, Present, and Future*, pp. 8-9.

[198] Donna L. Washington, Elizabeth M. Yano, and James McGuire, et al., "Risk Factors for
Homelessness among Women Veterans," *Journal of Health Care for the Poor and
Underserved*, 21, no. 1 (January 2010), pp. 81-91.

[199] Jessica Wolfe et al., "Changing Demographic Characteristics of Women Veterans: Results
from a National Sample," *Military Medicine* 165, no. 10 (October 2000): 800.

[200] Rachel Kimerling, Amy E. Street, and Joanne Pavao, et al., "Military-Related Sexual Trauma
Among Veterans Health Administration Patients Returning From Afghanistan and Iraq,"
American Journal of Public Health, vol. 100, no. 8 (August 2010), pp. 1409-1412.

[201] Ibid., p. 1411. The study looked at both male and female veterans who had reported
experiencing military sexual trauma. The percentage of men who so reported was 0.7%.

[202] Ibid.

[203] Anne G. Sandler, Brenda M. Booth, Michelle A. Mengeling, and Bradley N. Doebbeling,
"Life Span and Repeated Violence Against Women During Military Service: Effects on
Health Status and Outpatient Utilization," *Journal of Women's Health* 13, no. 7 (2004):
800.

[204] *FY2010 AHAR Veterans Supplement*, p. 7.

[205] U.S. Department of Veterans Affairs, *Advisory Committee on Women Veterans Report 2010*,
September 2010, p. 6,http://www1.va.gov/WOMENVET/docs/ACWV_Report_2010.pdf.

[206] *Healthcare for Homeless Veterans Programs: Twenty-Third Annual Report*, Table 5-3, p. 202.

[207] *Twenty-First Annual Progress Report on the Domiciliary Care for Homeless Veterans Program*, p. 9.

[208] U.S. Government Accountability Office, *Homeless Women Veterans: Actions Needed to Ensure Safe and Appropriate Housing*, GAO-12-182, December 2011, p. 28, http://www.gao.gov/assets/590/587334.pdf.

[209] *Prevalence and Risk of Homelessness Among U.S. Veterans: A Multisite Investigation*, p. 25.

In: Veteran Housing Assistance   ISBN: 978-1-62417-369-1
Editor: Craig Del Monte   © 2013 Nova Science Publishers, Inc.

Chapter 3

VETERAN HOMELESSNESS: VA AND HUD ARE WORKING TO IMPROVE DATA ON SUPPORTIVE HOUSING PROGRAM*

United States Government Accountability Office

WHY GAO DID THIS STUDY

According to a HUD and VA report, veterans are overrepresented among the homeless population. The HUD-VASH program combines rental assistance for homeless veterans in the form of section 8 Housing Choice vouchers provided by HUD with case management and clinical services provided by VA at VAMCs and community-based outpatient clinics. This collaborative initiative between the two agencies is intended to target the most vulnerable, most needy, and chronically homeless veterans. GAO was asked to examine (1) how VA and HUD determine veteran eligibility for HUD-VASH, (2) what data VA and HUD collect and report on HUD-VASH and their data reliability efforts, and (3) what is known about HUD-VASH performance.

To address these objectives, GAO reviewed HUD-VASH program requirements and reported program data through March 2012; and interviewed VA and HUD headquarters officials, staff at a non-representative sample of 10

---

* This is an edited, reformatted and augmented version of the Highlights of GAO-12-726, a report to the Committee on Veterans' Affairs, House of Representatives, dated June 2012.

VAMCs and 10 PHAs, and representatives of organizations that advocate for veterans or individuals experiencing homelessness.

GAO makes no recommendations in this report. HUD, VA, and the U.S. Interagency Council on Homelessness generally agreed with GAO's conclusions.

WHAT GAO FOUND

The Department of Veterans Affairs (VA) and Department of Housing and Urban Development (HUD) rely on VA medical centers (VAMC) and public housing agencies (PHA) that serve veterans directly to determine participant eligibility for the HUD-VA Supportive Housing (HUD-VASH) program. VAMC staff GAO contacted said that they interview veterans interested in the HUD-VASH program to assess whether the veteran met the program's definition of homelessness, check VA's electronic patient record system to determine whether the veteran was eligible for VA health care, and obtain the veteran's agreement to participate in case management. VAMCs refer eligible veterans to partnering PHAs (subject to rental assistance voucher availability) and are required to place them on an interest list when no vouchers are available. PHA staff GAO contacted said that they compare the veteran's reported income to information provided by third-party sources, such as the Social Security Administration, to verify that the veteran's household income did not exceed HUD-VASH program limits and check state sex offender registries to help ensure that no member of the veteran's household was subject to a lifetime registration requirement.

VA and HUD collect various data on veteran participation and voucher utilization and are taking steps to address the reliability of data collected and reported on HUD-VASH. Since 2008, VA has used an electronic database referred to as the Dashboard to collect and report various data, such as the number of veterans issued a voucher and seeking housing and the number of veterans housed. VA described taking a number of steps intended to help ensure the reliability of Dashboard-based reports, including routine reviews of underlying reports. VA expects to fully implement reporting based on data collected with its new Homeless Operations Management and Evaluation System (HOMES) by July 2012. According to VA, HOMES incorporates additional data reliability controls, such as data fields that automatically limit responses to predefined ranges. HUD also collects data on HUD-VASH voucher utilization, although HUD officials acknowledged discrepancies between VA and HUD data. VA and HUD are working to finalize an information-sharing agreement intended to help the departments better identify the source of the discrepancies and validate reports based on HOMES data.

HUD-VASH data show that the program has moved previously homeless veterans into housing. As of March 2012, nearly 31,200 veterans lived in HUD-VASH supported housing (about 83 percent of the rental assistance vouchers authorized under the program). The program goal is to have veterans in housing represent 88 percent of authorized vouchers by September 2012; several states had met or exceeded the goal as of March 2012. VAMC and PHA staff GAO contacted also cited challenges in administering the HUD-VASH program, including a lack of resources to assist veterans with moving into housing. In April 2012, HUD released a best practices document that illustrated how some of the challenges identified had been addressed. For example, one PHA applied for county Community Development Block Grant funds to assist veterans with security and utility deposits.

ABBREVIATIONS

HOMES	Homeless Operations Management and Evaluation System
HUD	Department of Housing and Urban Development
HUD-VASH	Department of Housing and Urban Development and Veterans Affairs Supportive Housing
PHA	Public Housing Agency
PIC	Public and Indian Housing Information Center
OMB	Office of Management and Budget
VA	Department of Veterans Affairs
VAMC	Veterans Administration Medical Center
VISN	Veterans Integrated Service Network
VMS	Voucher Management System

June 26, 2012
The Honorable Jeff Miller
Chairman
The Honorable Bob Filner
Ranking Member
Committee on Veterans' Affairs
House of Representatives

According to a Department of Housing and Urban Development (HUD) and Department of Veterans Affairs (VA) report, veterans are overrepresented among the homeless population.[1] In 2010, they accounted for roughly 9.5 percent of the total adult population (over the age of 18) but 13 percent of homeless adults in shelters or transitional housing. The report also notes that veterans represented 16 percent of homeless adults at a given point in time.[2] The larger percentage of veterans identified during the point-in-time count may reflect the greater likelihood of chronic homelessness among veterans. Chronically homeless veterans include those who cycle between streets and shelters, have frequent episodes of homelessness, and struggle with physical or mental health problems.

VA and HUD, in collaboration with other federal agencies, are committed to preventing and ending veteran homelessness by 2015, and both departments fund several programs to house homeless veterans. The HUD-VA Supportive Housing (HUD-VASH) program, a collaborative initiative between HUD and VA, is intended to target the most vulnerable, most needy, and chronically homeless veterans. Its primary goal is to move veterans and their families out of homelessness and promote housing stability. HUD-VASH combines rental assistance for homeless veterans in the form of section 8 Housing Choice vouchers provided by HUD with case management and clinical services provided by VA at Veterans Administration Medical Centers (VAMC) and community-based outpatient clinics. HUD provides the vouchers through public housing agencies (PHA) that partner with eligible medical centers or other entities.[3] As of March 28, 2012, more than 35,800 HUD-VASH vouchers were in use.[4] HUD-VASH is the nation's largest permanent supportive housing initiative for veterans.

You requested that we review the HUD-VASH program, including compliance with statutory eligibility criteria, data integrity, and utilization of performance measures to track long-term outcomes. In this report, we examine (1) how VA and HUD determine that veterans who participate in the HUD-VASH program meet the statutory eligibility criteria, (2) what data VA and HUD collect and report on the HUD-VASH program and the steps that VA and HUD take to help ensure the reliability of these data, and (3) what is known about the performance of the HUD-VASH program.

In conducting this work, we reviewed VA and HUD documents that describe the purpose of the HUD-VASH program and the agencies' roles and responsibilities related to HUD-VASH. We reviewed eligibility requirements in the HUD-VASH statute and program manuals. We selected a purposive, non-representative sample of 10 locations in which to interview management and staff at VAMCs and their partnering PHAs. We asked VAMC and PHA staff about their procedures for administering HUD-VASH, including making eligibility determinations; cooperation at the local level; data they collect and report on HUD-VASH; and their perspectives on the program's effectiveness. We selected the 10 locations based on several criteria, including a significant presence of homeless veterans in and a large allocation of HUD-VASH vouchers to the state for fiscal years 2008 through 2010, identified best practices or challenges in administering the HUD-VASH program, and geographic diversity. To obtain information on the presence of homeless veterans by state, we reviewed the jointly developed veteran supplements to HUD's annual homeless reports for 2009 and 2010. We used information from HUD on annual HUD-VASH voucher allocations by PHA and partnering VAMC for fiscal years 2008 through 2010, as the program was expanded with funding for new vouchers in 2008. We also reviewed federal strategic plans that address veteran homelessness to obtain information on VA's and HUD's goals for reducing veteran homelessness. To determine what is known about the performance of the HUD-VASH program, we reviewed VA and HUD reports on HUD-VASH voucher utilization and other VA reports on the program. In addition, we interviewed representatives of, and gathered documentation from, HUD and VA headquarters; the U.S. Interagency Council on Homelessness (Interagency Council); and veteran and homeless advocacy organizations, including the National Coalition for Homeless Veterans, the National Coalition for the Homeless, the National Alliance to End Homelessness, and Vietnam Veterans of America. See appendix I for a more detailed discussion of our scope and methodology.

We conducted this performance audit from September 2011 through June 2012 in accordance with generally accepted government auditing standards. Those standards require that we plan and perform the audit to obtain sufficient, appropriate evidence to provide a reasonable basis for our findings and conclusions based on our audit objectives. We believe that the evidence obtained provides a reasonable basis for our findings and conclusions based on our audit objectives.

BACKGROUND

HUD and VA established HUD-VASH in 1992 to target veterans with severe psychiatric or substance use disorders. From fiscal years 1992 through 1994, the program provided approximately 1,753 housing vouchers to homeless veterans.[5] After the initial voucher distributions, no new vouchers were made available to homeless veterans until fiscal year 2008. From fiscal years 2008 through 2011, the program received funding for about 37,000 new HUD-VASH vouchers. As of fiscal year 2008, program participants are no longer required to have chronic mental illnesses or chronic substance use disorders with required treatment. However, a significant number of veterans with those issues are expected to be helped within the program's target population of veterans experiencing chronic homelessness.

Program Funding

Obligations for new HUD-VASH vouchers and supportive services increased from $78 million in fiscal year 2008 to $172 million in fiscal year 2011 (see figure 1).[6]

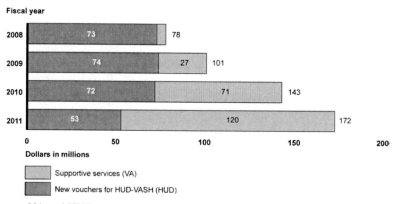

Source: VA and HUD.
Note: Totals may not add due to rounding.

Figure 1. HUD-VASH Program Obligations, Fiscal Years 2008 through 2011.

Administration of Assistance and Eligibility

As of April 2012, more than 140 VA facilities were participating in HUD-VASH.[7] In addition, according to HUD, more than 360 PHAs had partnered with VA facilities to administer HUD-VASH nationwide since fiscal year 2008.[8] The allocation process for HUD-VASH vouchers is a collaborative approach that relies on three sets of data to determine geographic need: HUD point-in-time data on homeless veterans needing services in the area, VAMC data on the number of contacts with homeless veterans, and performance data from PHAs and VAMCs. Based on this analysis of geographic need (adjusted by the number of vouchers received in previous years' allocations), HUD and VA identify communities that should receive VASH vouchers. The agencies then determine the exact number to allocate in proportion with each community's level of need. VA then identifies VAMCs from these communities to participate in HUD-VASH, taking into account VA's case management resources. HUD considers a PHA's administrative performance and in consultation with VA identifies PHAs located in the jurisdiction of the VAMCs and invites them to apply for HUD-VASH vouchers. The selected VAMCs and PHAs in a given community must partner to administer the program. Under certain terms, HUD allows PHAs to make a portion of their HUD-VASH vouchers project-based (that is, tied to a specific housing unit and not to a tenant). PHAs can request that a portion of their allocation of HUD-VASH vouchers be project-based as long as funding for those vouchers, when added to the funding for vouchers from the PHA's regular voucher program that have been project-based, does not exceed 20 percent of the PHA's overall voucher budget authority and the partnering VAMC supports the project.

The Veterans Health Administration within VA issues a HUD-VASH handbook, which establishes procedures and responsibilities for administering HUD-VASH. VA also has released a HUD-VASH Resource Guide that was developed in conjunction with other federal and community partners. It includes additional HUD-VASH guidance and provides technical assistance on clinical issues pertaining to individuals in permanent supportive housing programs.

HUD's policies and procedures for HUD-VASH, including PHA responsibilities, are defined in a *Federal Register* notice, the most recent of which dates to March 2012. Figure 2 illustrates the processes and activities for which VA and HUD (through PHAs in compliance with HUD regulations) are responsible when providing HUD-VASH assistance. For example, VA screens veterans to help ensure the following.

- That they are homeless based on the McKinney-Vento Homeless Assistance Act definition; that is generally, a person who lacks regular, adequate housing or will imminently lose housing and lacks resources to obtain other permanent housing.[9]

- That they are eligible for VA health care.[10]
- That they are willing to participate in case management services that are intended to promote housing stability and link the veteran to needed clinical services. According to VA, many veterans experiencing homelessness have physical, emotional, or other problems that make the goal of living independently challenging.

VAMCs refer veterans who meet VA requirements to PHAs, which determine eligibility based on HUD's income requirements for section 8. To be eligible for assistance, households generally must have very low incomes—not exceeding 50 percent of the area median income, as determined by HUD.[11] Except for a sex offender provision, HUD-VASH offers several waivers to the regular section 8 voucher requirements. Specifically, under HUD-VASH, PHAs cannot deny assistance to potentially eligible households for past section 8 violations, such as previous nonpayment, or for criminal history. However, no members of the veteran household can be subject to a lifetime registration requirement under a state registration program for sex offenders. Once the veteran meets HUD's requirements for the program, the PHA can issue the voucher for participation in HUD-VASH.

Data Collection, Analysis, Reporting, and Systems

According to VA, the agency has assumed primary responsibility for collecting and reporting HUD-VASH data, which it does for internal performance purposes, monthly congressional reporting, and compliance with Office of Management and Budget (OMB) reporting. VA and HUD officials told us that VA also provides HUD with program data, which HUD uses for internal performance purposes and for OMB reporting.

More than one VA office shares responsibilities for HUD-VASH data collection and analysis. VA's National Center for Homelessness among Veterans (national center), which falls under the National Homeless Program Office, undertakes development and evaluation of care options and research and methodology related to VA's homeless programs. Additionally, VA's Northeast Program Evaluation Center supports and oversees data collection for VA's mental health programs. According to a VA official, this center provides sites with day-to-day support on technical aspects of data collection, and the national center provides specific feedback on the data collection process and analysis, among other activities.

| Initial intake | Initial case management | Housing assistance processing | Continuing support |

Initial intake

Screening for VA eligibility and suitability, providing orientation

Initial case management

Accepting veteran into program, reserving voucher, and referring veteran to PHA

Housing assistance processing

Providing case management and assisting with housing placement process

Screening for HUD eligibility, assigning voucher, and processing housing assistance request

Continuing support

Providing ongoing case management

Providing ongoing rental assistance payments

VA
HUD (PHA)

Source: VA and Federal Register.
Note: HUD provides funding for the program, but HUD-VASH administration at the local level is carried out by PHAs.

Figure 2. VA and HUD Responsibilities during Provision of HUD-VASH Assistance.

VA currently uses two systems to collect HUD-VASH program information. According to VA, in 2008, it implemented a HUD-VASH database, referred to as the Dashboard, to collect monthly program status updates from HUD-VASH sites. VAMC staff submit Dashboard reports to their respective Veterans Integrated Service Networks (VISN), which in turn submit facility-level reports to the national center.[12] VA officials told us that VA implemented a new data collection system, the Homeless Operations Management and Evaluation System (HOMES), in April 2011, and VA is in the process of fully implementing reporting mechanisms required to generate reports based on HOMES data.[13] HOMES collects information for several of VA's homeless programs, including HUD-VASH. It is designed to track and maintain data on individual veterans as they move through VA's system of care, including HUD-VASH participation. For example, VA's HOMES user manual states that a HUD-VASH clinician who is familiar with the veteran should complete and submit a HUD-VASH monthly status report form for veterans currently enrolled in the program. The report is intended to capture various information on the veteran for the past 30-day period, including the number of contacts the veteran had for case management, the veteran's housing arrangement, amount and source of any income, visits to the emergency room or other hospitalizations (including those for mental health conditions), use of alcohol or illegal drugs, and satisfaction (including with their current accommodations, safety of living, and leisure activities).

According to HUD officials, as part of its section 8 program, HUD collects voucher utilization and household information using two information systems, the Voucher Management System (VMS) and Public and Indian Housing Information Center (PIC). PHAs are responsible for submitting VMS and PIC data to HUD. HUD uses VMS as a centralized system to monitor and manage PHAs' use of vouchers. VMS data include PHAs' monthly leasing and expenses for HUD-VASH vouchers, which HUD uses to obligate and disburse PHA funding. PHAs enter voucher totals in VMS rather than individual records of HUD-VASH voucher activity. HUD uses PIC as a centralized system to track information on households assisted and lease activity. PIC data fields include PHA identification, assistance program type (such as HUD-VASH), and household demographic information. PIC data fields also include information on income sources and amounts, assets, rent, housing type, and whether the subsidy is tenant-based or project-based.

HUD-VASH ELIGIBILITY IS DETERMINED AT THE LOCAL LEVEL

According to VA and HUD, the departments rely on VAMCs and PHAs to make determinations on veteran eligibility for the HUD-VASH program. Based on our meetings with staff at 10 VAMCs and 10 PHAs nationwide, VAMCs and PHAs generally followed the same procedures to determine that veterans met statutory requirements.

Initial Screening Determines whether Veterans Meet VA Requirements

VAMC staff that we contacted described how they screened veterans to determine whether they met requirements for HUD-VASH.

- **Homeless status:** To verify that a veteran met the McKinney-Vento definition of "homeless," VAMC staff told us that they interviewed the veteran. This included, for example, discussing the veteran's current housing situation (homeless, precariously housed, doubled up, in own housing but facing housing loss/eviction, or stably housed), and history or pattern of housing stability/instability. Some VAMC staff also told us that community organizations referring veterans into the HUD-VASH program may provide documentation supporting the veteran's homeless status.
- **VA health care:** To verify that a veteran is eligible for VA health care, VAMC staff in several locations told us that they determined if the individual had an existing record in VA's electronic patient record system. VA determines VA health care eligibility based on whether the individual meets the definition of veteran, has a minimum period of active duty service, and is enrolled in the VA health care system. A dishonorable discharge generally disqualifies an individual from receiving VA benefits.
- **Case management:** According to VAMC staff, a psychosocial assessment, which evaluates the veteran's clinical and service needs, helps them to determine an appropriate level of case management for each veteran. This involves considering whether the veteran has (1) complex service needs or health conditions, such as serious mental

illness or substance use disorder; (2) nonchronic service needs that could be overcome or managed with treatment; or (3) few or minor service needs and is employable. Prior to enrollment in HUD-VASH, each veteran must agree to participate in case management. According to VA guidance, case managers must document the veteran's HUD-VASH enrollment using a HOMES form. For veterans who do not enter the program, the form lists reasons the veteran did not enter, including the veteran's refusal to agree with the terms of the program (case management). In Los Angeles, New York, Washington, D.C., and Wyoming, VAMC staff explained that they required veterans to sign a case management agreement. VA officials told us that this was a local management practice rather than a requirement based on the HUD-VASH handbook. Following enrollment, the case manager and the veteran work together to develop an individualized treatment plan with goals that are revisited over the course of the veteran's participation in HUD-VASH. VA views case management as a key component of HUD-VASH and its case management services are intended to help improve the veteran's physical and mental health and enhance the veteran's housing stability. Additionally, VA's case management aims to support recoveries from physical and mental illness and substance use disorders. According to VA, HUD-VASH does not require veterans to be sober prior to program enrollment; however, the veteran's treatment plan is recovery-focused and incorporates his or her recovery goals. In addition to monitoring the veteran's treatment plan, the role of the case manager involves helping the veteran to access other medical and behavioral treatment resources as needed.

VA regards failure to participate in case management as grounds for termination or denial of program participation. However, several VAMC staff told us that VA makes every effort to re-engage veterans in case management before proceeding with termination for nonparticipation. If VA determines that the veteran no longer requires case management services, the veteran may continue to receive the HUD-VASH housing subsidy.

In such cases, the VA case manager should notify the PHA that case management is no longer required but that the veteran's eligibility for a housing voucher remains unchanged. If the PHA has a voucher available in its regular section 8 program, the PHA can offer that voucher to the veteran and make the HUD-VASH voucher available to another homeless veteran.

As previously noted, VA refers veterans who meet its requirements for HUD-VASH to PHAs, subject to voucher availability. The HUD-VASH handbook requires that if there are no available case management openings or vouchers, HUD-VASH program staff place the veteran on an interest list. According to VA, this list consists of all individuals who have been in contact with HUD-VASH staff and expressed interest in the program. These persons are subsequently screened for eligibility and a determination is made regarding acceptance. If a veteran is not eligible but vouchers are available, staff would make a referral to other VA or community resources. If a veteran is eligible but no vouchers are available, program staff must document the reason for denial in HOMES as lack of voucher availability.

As of March 28, 2012, VA data show that an estimated 1,689 or 4 percent of the HUD-VASH vouchers authorized nationwide were available for use. Of the 10 VAMCs we contacted, 6 had vouchers available for use as of March 28, 2012, including the Bronx (New York) VAMC with an estimated 63 vouchers available for use and the Seattle VAMC with an estimated 32 vouchers available for use.

The other four VAMCs had fewer than five remaining vouchers as of the same date. Regarding interest lists, staff at the Washington, D.C. VAMC told us that there were about 1,000 veterans on their facility's interest list. The staff also told us that they had developed a screening tool to help make acceptance decisions and prioritize remaining vouchers for veterans on their interest list.

According to VA, in addition to targeting chronically homeless veterans, consideration for HUD-VASH enrollment also may be given to women, families with children, disabled veterans, and those who served in Operations Iraqi Freedom and New Dawn in Iraq and Operation Enduring Freedom in Afghanistan.

VAMC staff we contacted generally told us that they routinely directed veterans screened for HUD-VASH to other suitable VA programs, including VA's Grant and Per Diem and Domiciliary Care for Homeless Veterans programs.[14] For example, the staff explained that they might refer veterans to other VA programs pending HUD-VASH acceptance if another program was more immediately appropriate for the veteran or if the veteran needed services not available under HUD-VASH (such as dental care). Some VAMC staff also mentioned local resources as another referral option.

PHAs Conduct Additional Screening on Income and Other Requirements

PHA staff that we contacted described how they screened veterans to determine whether they met income and other requirements after receiving a referral from the VAMC.

- **Income:** PHA staff told us that they generally relied on third-party sources, such as the Social Security or Veterans Benefits administrations, to verify the reported income of HUD-VASH applicants. HUD requires PHAs to include certain sources of household income in determining income eligibility, including earned and benefits-related income. The HUD-VASH voucher subsidizes recipients' rental payments and applicants must provide proof that their income level qualifies for this assistance.
- **State sex offender registry status:** PHA staff told us that they checked the sex offender registry for all members of the veteran household who were at least 18. In New York, the PHA staff informed us that they checked for all household members over 16 in compliance with the age limit for that state. If the veteran was subject to lifetime registration under a state registration program for sex offenders, the PHA would refuse the voucher application. If a family member who intended to occupy the assisted unit was subject to lifetime registration under such a program, the application would proceed only if that individual was removed permanently from the household.

To familiarize veterans approved for a HUD-VASH voucher with the PHA's requirements for HUD-VASH, staff at some PHAs we contacted told us that they conducted briefings with veterans. In several locations, PHAs held such briefings in a group format. Staff at PHAs with a smaller number of HUD-VASH vouchers sometimes met one-on-one with veterans.

Once the veteran is in housing, PHAs reverify income and complete a housing unit inspection, typically on an annual basis. Some PHAs may conduct recertification procedures less frequently.[15] One of the PHAs in our sample was in this category and conducted recipient renewals annually or biannually on a case-by-case basis. The PHA can terminate assistance when a veteran has been evicted from a unit or for serious and repeated lease violations. However, prior to terminating any section 8 participant, PHAs must provide the opportunity for an informal hearing. According to HUD officials, as part of HUD's routine review of PHA records (such as to determine the accuracy of family income and rent calculations), HUD may review HUD-VASH tenant files if the files are included in a larger sample, but such reviews are not specific to the HUD-VASH program.

BOTH VA AND HUD HAVE BEEN TAKING STEPS TO ADDRESS DATA RELIABILITY

VA Provides the Primary Data for HUD-VASH Reporting

Both VA and HUD report on HUD-VASH using information from VA's Dashboard database. VA uses the Dashboard to collect summary count information from VAMCs and provides monthly Dashboard-based reports to HUD and Congress. Those reports typically include several data elements or measures on voucher utilization, including the number of veterans issued a voucher and looking for housing and the number of veterans housed (under lease). See table 1 for additional Dashboard data elements.

Table 1. HUD-VASH Program Measures That VA Collects in Dashboard System and Reports

Data element	Description
Total vouchers authorized and appropriated	Total number of vouchers allocated to each PHA partnering with the VAMC facility since fiscal year 2008
Vouchers currently in use	Total number of vouchers either reserved for or issued to a veteran
Vouchers reserved for veterans who are undergoing PHA validation	Number of vouchers VAMC has reserved for veterans who have been referred to a participating PHA for voucher application processing
Vouchers issued to veterans who are actively seeking a lease	Number of veterans already awarded a voucher by a PHA and who are currently seeking housing
Current veterans housed/ under lease	Number of veterans awarded a voucher by a PHA and living in PHA-approved housing

Source: VA.

In addition to the Dashboard, VA uses HOMES to collect data on veterans. HOMES data reflect a series of electronic forms that case managers must complete from the time a veteran is screened for the program to the time a veteran leaves the program. Although HOMES data could be used to create the information captured in the Dashboard database, VA has not yet completed development and testing of report-generating mechanisms necessary to release reports based on HOMES data, according to VA officials. VA officials also told us that they intended to begin using HOMES data for congressional reporting purposes by July 2012 and eventually discontinue the Dashboard reporting mechanism.

VA Has Taken a Number of Steps to Help Ensure Data Reliability

VA has taken a number of steps to help ensure the reliability of HUD-VASH data reported though the Dashboard database. We compared VA's processes against standards for internal control, including, among other things, having processes and procedures that provide reasonable assurance of the reliability of reports for internal and external use by

- establishing and supporting a control environment with clearly defined areas of responsibility and appropriate lines of reporting,
- incorporating controls over information processing, and
- monitoring performance measures and indicators.[16]

HUD-VASH reporting responsibilities, as identified in VA's guidance, appeared to be consistent with HUD-VASH program responsibilities. For instance, case managers collect and submit HUD-VASH evaluation data on veterans. HUD-VASH program coordinators are responsible for conducting appropriate audits of performance measures. VAMC facility directors are responsible for verifying that staff provide timely reporting of veteran activity. Finally, the VISN's homeless coordinators are responsible for helping ensure that data are submitted in a timely manner and the VISN directors are responsible for helping ensure the accuracy of these data.

According to VA officials, the national center reviews individual weekly Dashboard reports from VISNs for reasonableness by comparing submissions with prior week reports. Questions or concerns are addressed to the respective VISN and the national center corrects weekly reports accordingly.

As discussed previously, Dashboard reports include a number of program performance measures, including a specific measure for the program's goal of moving veterans out of homelessness (the number of veterans under lease). In addition to providing data for external reporting, VA officials told us that the

Dashboard database serves as a program management tool. According to VA officials, the national center uses the Dashboard reports to monitor program status at individual sites and also compares program performance across sites.

VA also has taken a number of steps to help ensure the reliability of HUD-VASH data collected through HOMES. Consistent with standards for internal control, HOMES reporting responsibilities are clearly defined in VA guidance and, according to VA officials, HOMES data are collected for individual veterans as opposed to the Dashboard's facility-level counts that did not identify individuals. HOMES includes a number of additional controls. For example, electronic data checks incorporated into HOMES improve data validity and reduce the risk of errors. Authorized program service providers enter program and veteran information into HOMES but, where appropriate, certain data fields automatically limit responses to predefined data ranges to reduce data entry errors. According to VA officials, the system is capable of flagging records for review based on approximate matches of name or Social Security number. Furthermore, only certain authorized users may edit records after data are submitted.

VA and HUD Have been Taking Steps to Reduce Data Discrepancies

Although counts of voucher use generated from HUD's and VA's information systems produce different totals, a proposed information-sharing agreement between HUD and VA is intended to facilitate data sharing and identify and resolve discrepancies. HUD has compared VA data with its VMS and PIC data for the purpose of validating HUD-VASH data.[17] Validating data (in this case, Dashboard data) with an independent data source (such as HUD data) is an additional standard for internal control. HUD collects some HUD-VASH data, including the number of veterans receiving housing assistance (veterans under lease) through its VMS and PIC systems, but generally does not use these data for HUD-VASH reporting purposes. According to HUD and VA officials, both departments consistently use Dashboard data for reporting purposes.

HUD provided its analysis of VA, VMS, and PIC data comparisons of vouchers under lease. For November 2011, HUD's analysis listed three totals for vouchers under lease: 27,159 vouchers according to VMS, 24,768 vouchers according to PIC, and 27,285 vouchers according to VA data. The totals also differed when HUD compared voucher counts at individual PHAs for the same month. HUD noted three totals for vouchers under lease at the Harrisburg Housing Authority: 19 vouchers according to VMS, 33 according to PIC, and 34 according to VA data. In another example, HUD noted three totals for vouchers under lease at the Housing Authority of Waco: 116 vouchers according to VMS, 13 according to PIC, and 119 according to VA data.

According to HUD officials, data discrepancies between VA and HUD data may have been due to one or more factors, assuming VA data provided at that time were accurate.

- First, PHAs may have incorrectly or inaccurately entered PIC or VMS data that relate to HUD-VASH participation counts.
- Second, PIC and VMS use different methodologies for assigning HUD-VASH voucher counts when veterans move across PHA jurisdictions, which could affect comparisons of participation data at the facility level. Under the HUD-VASH program, a veteran may use a HUD-VASH voucher in a jurisdiction outside of the PHA that initially awarded the voucher.[18] VMS voucher counts are associated with the initial voucher allocation site, regardless of the participating veteran's current location. PIC counts veteran households assisted and associates those counts with the veteran's current location.
- Third, in comparison with VA reporting, HUD has taken longer to make data available for analysis. For example, up to 80 days may elapse from the time a PHA must submit VMS data to the time that VMS information is available for analysis. According to VA, the agency typically has provided Dashboard data to Congress within 50 days after the end of each reporting month.

HUD's VMS and VA's Dashboard data are comparable when veteran participation is categorized by location; however, these respective data sources are not tied to personally identifying information. Therefore, the agencies have a difficult time identifying the specific source of data discrepancies. A proposed information-sharing agreement between HUD and VA is intended to facilitate record-level data sharing between the agencies and allow them to precisely identify and resolve data discrepancies between HUD's PIC data and VA's HOMES data. According to VA officials, once VA fully implements new reporting mechanisms, HOMES data will enable VA to provide summary status reports and identify information for veteran records used to create the summary totals. Further, they said that the agreement will allow VA to provide

HUD with HUD-VASH data including the participating VAMC and PHA, and personally identifying information for each veteran. According to HUD officials, HUD intends to compare these records with PIC data (which include personally identifying information) and then the agencies plan to coordinate with field offices to resolve discrepancies. As of June 2012, the information-sharing agreement was under review. The agencies expected to complete final revisions to the agreement by June 25, 2012 and execute the agreement by August 2012. If VA fully implements HOMES as a data source for reporting purposes and the agencies execute the agreement as planned, it would allow the agencies to match case records in the event of data discrepancies. Although the agreement is not expected to affect VA's monthly report submissions to Congress, according to the agencies, the information-sharing agreement should further improve their ability to validate HUD-VASH data on an ongoing basis.

HUD-VASH DATA SHOW THE PROGRAM HAS MOVED VETERANS INTO HOUSING

HUD-VASH Performance

Information VA reports for the HUD-VASH program has focused on voucher utilization (such as the number of veterans housed), but HOMES is supposed to provide VA with additional data on veteran outcomes. VA currently reports a number of measures (or various data) related to voucher utilization in monthly reports to Congress (see table 2).

Table 2. HUD-VASH Measures on Voucher Utilization (as of March 28, 2012)

Measure	Number	Percentage (of vouchers authorized)
Vouchers authorized	37,552	
Veterans in housing	31,197	83
Vouchers issued to veterans actively seeking a lease	4,046	11
Vouchers reserved for veterans undergoing PHA validation	620	2
Vouchers available for use	1,689	4

Source: VA.

These measures show that HUD-VASH has moved veterans out of homelessness. Nearly 31,200 veterans lived in HUD-VASH-supported housing as of March 28, 2012; veterans in housing represented about 83 percent of the vouchers authorized under the program. In addition, PHAs issued 4,046 vouchers to veterans who were actively seeking a lease and VAMCs reserved 620 vouchers for veterans undergoing PHA validation as of the same date. According to VA, the department's goal is for veterans in housing to represent at least 88 percent of authorized HUD-VASH vouchers by September 30, 2012. As figure 3 shows, several states had achieved or nearly achieved this goal as of March 2012, including the four states with the largest number of vouchers authorized—California, Florida, New York, and Texas.

For the 10 VAMCs we contacted, the percentage of veterans in housing varied, ranging from 70 percent to 95 percent as of March 28, 2012. For VAMCs further from the goal, such as the Sheridan VAMC in Wyoming (70 percent in housing), challenges with getting veterans placed in housing may be related to local housing markets. For example, Sheridan VAMC staff told us that there was a lack of affordable housing in the area. Similarly, staff at Greater Los Angeles Health Care System (79 percent in housing) told us that suitable housing stock (meeting program requirements for cost and housing quality) was limited, particularly in the West Los Angeles area where the VAMC facility is located. VA data show that both VAMCs had assigned 100 percent of their authorized vouchers to a veteran as of March 2012. However, nearly 30 percent of the Sheridan VAMC's vouchers and 21 percent of the Greater Los Angeles Health Care System's vouchers were assigned to veterans actively seeking housing at that time. We discuss challenges with getting veterans placed in housing in greater detail later in this report.

In October 2011, VA submitted a report to Congress that provides additional descriptive and performance-related information on HUD-VASH for June 2008 through September 2010. Summary information from the report includes

- characteristics of veterans admitted to the program;
- average number of days at each stage of the admission and housing process;
- veterans' typical 90-day housing situation within 3, 6, and 12 months of beginning case management; and
- reasons for ending case management.

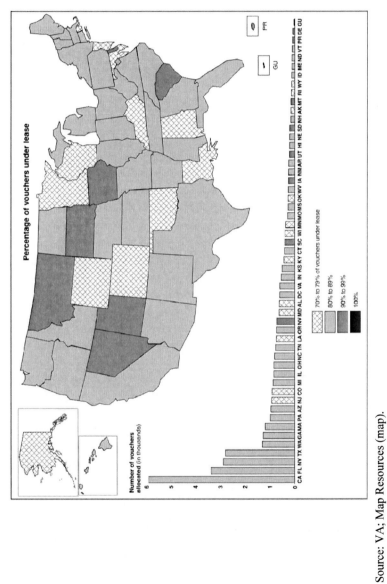

Source: VA; Map Resources (map).

Figure 3. HUD-VASH Voucher Allocations and Percentage of Vouchers under Lease by State, as of March 28, 2012.

For example, according to VA, for veterans who completed the housing process, the time frame from initial referral to HUD-VASH to the move into permanent housing averaged 130 days.

VA has plans to report additional information, such as measures of the time it took to complete various processes within the program (see table 3). In December 2011, VA issued guidance to its service networks outlining several outcome measures and related targets for which the department planned to start collecting data in fiscal year 2012.

VA also recently began conducting research (although not always nationwide) related to (1) the Housing First approach to supportive housing; (2) positive and negative outcomes for veterans who leave the HUD-VASH program; and (3) various case management approaches for treating veterans for substance abuse.[19] VA officials told us that they intend to use the results of these studies to assess operations and update policies and procedures accordingly, and to offer guidance on innovative practices to VAMCs. In June 2012, VA officials provided us with updates on these studies:

- Based on piloting the Housing First approach in Washington, D.C.'s HUD-VASH program in fiscal year 2009, VA determined that Housing First yielded several positive outcomes. The study compared results for 105 HUD-VASH vouchers set aside for Housing First and 70 vouchers that followed VA's usual treatment process. VA found that, under Housing First, veteran placement into housing took, on average, 35 days from admission, compared with 223 days under the usual treatment process. Additionally, under Housing First, a reduced proportion of veterans had used emergency room and inpatient mental health services, and the housing retention rate was 98 percent after 1 year, compared with 86 percent under the usual treatment process. The pilot was expanded to 13 additional sites in fiscal year 2012, with VA and HUD monitoring for 3 years. Each site had 50 vouchers set aside for Housing First.

- Based on program data available at the end of June 2011, VA analyzed veterans who were already housed and left HUD-VASH for reasons categorized as positive (such as accomplishing goals or no longer needing program supports), negative (such as failing to comply with program requirements or being evicted), and neutral (such as death, illness, or transferring to another program site). According to VA, within the sample, 37 percent of exits were positive, 23 percent were negative, 30 percent were neutral, and there were insufficient data for 10 percent of exits. VA officials told us that VA and HUD will work together to conduct a more in-depth study of veterans leaving the program for adverse reasons to identify the major factors involved. The officials informed us that as of March 2012, the departments were in the process of obtaining OMB approval to follow up with veterans who had left HUD-VASH.

- VA has launched a 3-site research study comparing the effectiveness of four different intervention methods for veterans with substance use disorders and mental health problems. Methods tested will include standard case management, intensive case management, tele-coaching, and electronic interactive practices. As of June 2012, VA officials told us that they had begun interviewing veterans to participate in the study. VA did not expect results to be available until 2013.

HUD-VASH case managers have started to complete a monthly status form in HOMES that includes data on outcomes. For example, case managers must record (1) changes in the veteran's community adjustment and social contacts; (2) hospitalizations for unscheduled medical conditions or mental health conditions; (3) employment status and other sources of income or benefits; and (4) use of alcohol or illegal drugs, using a clinical rating scale. In addition to the monthly status form, case managers are required to complete in HOMES a HUD-VASH exit form for each veteran who is discharged from the program. The exit form includes some of the indicators in the monthly report, the veteran's status upon discharge, and the reason for exit.

Table 3. Selected HUD-VASH Outcome Metrics, 2011

Performance metric	Target
Time frame to make decision on acceptance into HUD-VASH program	Within 3 working days of referral
Time frame to refer veteran to PHA once accepted into HUD-VASH program	Within 15 days of acceptance into the program
Time frame from acceptance into HUD-VASH program to placement in housing	Within 100 days of acceptance into the program
Percentage of discharges from HUD-VASH program for adverse reasons	10 percent or less

Source: VA.

Housing stability for veterans participating in HUD-VASH is a component of the program's primary goal, along with moving those veterans out of homelessness and into housing. VA's case management efforts play an integral role in helping veterans to achieve housing stability. VA's current monthly reports, which show the number of veterans housed under the program, do not address housing stability. However, VA's October 2011 report to Congress gave some indication of general voucher turnover and housing tenure. More specifically, the report showed the number and percentage of veterans leaving the program for positive and negative reasons at various stages of the housing process. It also showed veterans' typical housing situation over the previous 90 days after 3, 6, and 12 months of participation. Beginning in April 2011, VA told us that case managers began using HOMES to record information on HUD-VASH participants. This would include entering information on each veteran's housing situation upon enrollment, every 30 days following enrollment, and upon exit from the program. While not enough time has passed to assess the reporting related to HOMES data, VA expects it to provide a range of useful data for site monitoring and program management. Along with other data expected to be collected in HOMES, detailed information on veterans' housing situation every 30 days should provide VA with an opportunity to assess program performance in helping veterans to achieve housing stability.

HUD Has Disseminated Strategies to Address Some Program Challenges

Based on our interviews at 10 VAMCs and partnering PHAs, staff frequently cited four challenges relating to program administration or processes that they perceived as negatively affecting the goal of housing homeless veterans and helping them maintain housing stability.

Delayed VAMC referrals to the PHA. As previously noted, for fiscal year 2012, VA's goal is for VAMCs to refer veterans accepted into HUD-VASH to the PHA within 15 days of acceptance into the program. However, PHA staff discussed challenges associated with receiving timely HUD-VASH referrals from the partnering VAMC, particularly at the beginning of a new allocation year. In 9 of the 10 locations, PHA staff told us that delayed referrals from VA slowed the voucher utilization process. While PHAs generally can begin accepting referrals once HUD awards the vouchers, delayed referrals from VA extended the time frame between a PHA receiving the vouchers and getting the voucher holder into housing. Staff at King County Housing Authority in Seattle suggested that VA's initial delay in making

HUD-VASH referrals was related to VA needing to hire and assign case managers, while HUD could move quickly to pass funding on to the PHAs to issue vouchers. Staff at two VAMCs acknowledged the challenge in making initial referrals to the PHA. In one location, the staff explained that to provide an adequate number of case managers, they would need to know how many new vouchers had been added and, therefore, how many new HUD-VASH veterans they would need to serve. Moreover, once new case managers were hired, they had to undergo training and orientation, resulting in additional delays. Staff in several PHA locations noted that VAMC referral time frames had been improving.

HUD-VASH case manager workload. VA's goal is to have a ratio of 1 case manager to 25 veterans. However, when we contacted VAMCs in January and February 2012, several VAMC staff told us that some case managers had 40 or more cases, as the following examples illustrate:

- In South Dakota, staff at the Meade County Housing and Redevelopment Commission expressed general concern that the workload for the case manager serving their area may have been unreasonable or otherwise impractical. According to staff at Black Hills Health Care System, which partners with the housing authority, the case manager assigned to Meade County and other locations managed 51 cases in total.
- Similarly, case managers at James A. Haley VAMC in Tampa had between 45 and 50 cases. Staff at the Tampa Housing Authority told us that more intensive case management could reduce or eliminate veteran terminations from HUD-VASH due to nonpayment or other violations of the housing agreement.
- Staff at Greater Los Angeles Health Care System told us that efforts were under way to reduce their average caseload of 45 per case manager. The facility was accepting applications for additional case managers and also planning to contract with an external entity to supplement case management services.

VA has made efforts to address staffing at its VAMCs, and when we later contacted two of the VAMCs identified with challenges, the staff told us that hiring additional case managers had reduced their caseloads significantly. Additionally, VA provided us with a report on HUD-VASH program hiring as of February 29, 2012. The report showed that 95 percent of program positions across all VISNs were filled. Among the VAMCs we contacted, the percentage of HUD-VASH positions filled ranged from 50 percent to 100 percent. Case managers represent the majority of HUD-VASH positions, but some facilities have also hired clinical supervisors, substance use disorder specialists, peer support and housing specialists, and other program support staff.

Identifying housing for veterans. Staff at VAMCs in several locations told us that veterans experienced challenges with finding housing. In Wyoming, the VAMC staff explained that the market for affordable housing was tight in Casper and Sheridan, areas served by the VAMC. Additionally, they said that the partnering PHA that served Sheridan recently reduced the maximum allowable housing assistance payment from $595 to $571 and this amount limited access to decent housing in the area. The staff added that many landlords also have been reluctant to rent to veterans with criminal histories. VAMC staff in South Dakota similarly noted that a partnering PHA had decreased the housing allowance for the area it served while some landlords had increased their rents. They explained that they used communications with a local homeless coalition, community stakeholders, and landlords to identify options for affordable housing. At Greater Los Angeles Health Care System, the staff told us that a housing specialist had been hired and kept staff informed of new housing stock while working with developers and realtors to identify suitable housing. According to the VAMC staff, the housing specialist also has conducted outreach to educate landlords on HUD-VASH and advocate for veterans, making them aware that case management will be available to HUD-VASH tenants.

Move-in resources for veterans. Both PHA and VAMC staff discussed challenges veterans experience accessing the funds and household items that they needed to move in once they found a suitable housing unit. In some instances, veterans were delayed in moving into their units because of a lack of available funds to pay rental application fees, security deposits for rent or utilities, and the first month's rent. Such delays could affect VA's goal for placing veterans into housing within 100 days of being accepted into the program.

The availability of resources to help veterans varied among locations, but generally was more limited outside of larger cities. Two of the 10 locations had a consistent source that could provide this type of assistance to veterans. For example, New York City has a Department of Homeless Services that provides a range of services to homeless individuals. Through this entity, HUD-VASH veterans could receive assistance with security deposits, first month's rent, and household items. In Seattle, HUD-VASH veterans could access a limited-term Human Services and Veterans Levy that assisted veterans, military personnel and their families, and others in need through a variety of housing and supportive services. In other locations, VAMC and PHA staff told us that veterans had relied on local public or nonprofit assistance and on Homeless Prevention and Rapid Re-Housing Program funds that were temporarily provided under the Recovery Act.[20] Additionally, several said that they hoped veterans would be able to use funds that would be provided under the new Supportive Services for Veteran Families grant program.[21] Homeless Prevention and Rapid Re-Housing Program funds are no longer available and the other sources mentioned, according to the staff, often were insufficient or were not guaranteed. In some locations, the VAMC staff had developed other approaches to mitigating this challenge for veterans. For example, at several facilities, including Greater Los Angeles Health Care System, Black Hills Health Care System in South Dakota, and Washington, D.C. VAMC, the staff explained that they solicited landlords' cooperation in waiving or spreading out up-front fees. Additionally, staff at White River Junction VAMC in Vermont had developed a handbook for veterans participating in VA's homeless programs that included a community resources guide. They explained that the guide was included to assist veterans with obtaining furniture, household items, and other resources they needed to move into housing.

In April 2012, HUD released a best practices document that included practices submitted by PHAs and VAMCs that administer HUD-VASH. According to HUD, the purpose of the document is to share effective strategies for administering HUD-VASH and highlight the efforts of specific sites and other partners. According to HUD officials, VA was involved in soliciting best practices from VAMCs and reviewed the document that HUD developed. HUD intends to revise the document over time. While the document was developed from the housing standpoint, it includes information on strategies for carrying out procedures pertaining to general PHA and VAMC management. More specifically, it describes the ways in which individual sites have addressed specific challenges such as those identified previously. For example, in addition to the Los Angeles VAMC hiring a housing specialist, the document described other facilities' efforts to direct veterans to suitable housing by contracting with a nonprofit housing referral organization, maintaining a list of potential housing options in the VAMC's service area, and conducting targeted landlord outreach. Similarly, several PHAs had established a loan fund or trust fund to assist veterans with move-in costs, and one PHA applied for county Community Development Block Grant funds to assist veterans with security and utility deposits.

Advocacy Organizations Generally Shared Positive Views of HUD-VASH and Also Suggested Program Improvements

Advocates for veterans and the homeless that we contacted generally agreed that HUD-VASH was essential in helping homeless veterans to access housing and long-term treatment. Representatives at one of the organizations stated that the long-term housing HUD-VASH provides was crucial to addressing the immediate and long-term needs of homeless individuals and that combining case management with housing was appropriate for veterans with the most significant problems. Additionally, representatives at two organizations told us that HUD and VA sharing a common strategic goal had been beneficial and that program administrators had been responsive to the HUD-VASH community. Moreover, they noted that the program's administration had improved over time. Specifically, they explained that VA had been willing to make changes to improve HUD-VASH, including in terms of leadership. The advocates offered suggestions for improving the HUD-VASH program, including the following.

- One advocate suggested that the program should continue to target those with the greatest need for assistance and explore flexibility for service delivery mechanisms, including having case managers conduct more work in communities and outside of the traditional VAMC appointment approach. Related to this point, recently the Veterans Health Administration Homeless Program National Director noted that VA was taking steps to have more of a presence in the community. This included hiring HUD-VASH case managers living in communities where veterans were being served and seeking more opportunities to have case managers co-located with community-based organizations.
- A second advocate thought it would be useful to remove the section 8 limits on project-based housing under HUD-VASH to allow developers to allocate portions of higher-quality, mixed-use developments for project-based HUD-VASH vouchers. The

representative explained that this would be particularly helpful in locales with limited affordable housing and in areas that are desirable (particularly for female veterans with dependent children). HUD officials clarified that PHAs can make the case to HUD to have funding for project-based HUD-VASH vouchers exceed the voucher budget authority limit of 20 percent.[22] According to HUD officials, exceeding the limit must be tied to effective administration of HUD-VASH, and HUD had not received any such requests as of May 2012.

- A third advocate expressed that VA should increase its outreach to veteran service organizations to advertise to veterans who may not be participating in VA programs. VA officials told us that VA has a national outreach initiative under way that includes collaborating with veteran service organizations to make information on HUD-VASH and other VA programs more readily available.

- Finally, a fourth advocate emphasized that sufficient resources needed to be committed to HUD-VASH in support of the goal of ending veteran homelessness. The representative explained that a certain volume of vouchers needed to be in the system for it to be successful and that inconsistent resources led to uncertainty among service providers and veterans who need to access the program.

AGENCY COMMENTS

We provided a draft of this report to the Secretary of Housing and Urban Development, the Secretary of Veterans Affairs, and the Executive Director of the U.S. Interagency Council on Homelessness. We received comments from HUD, VA, and the Interagency Council HUD and VA also provided technical comments, which we incorporated in the report as appropriate. In their responses, HUD, VA, and the Interagency Council generally agreed with our conclusions. HUD and VA noted that they were committed to their partnership and the continued improvement of the HUD-VASH program. The Interagency Council stated in its response that VA and HUD work closely on local implementation through VA medical centers and public housing agencies, and have improved lease-up rates, enhanced data collection, and reduced the amount of time it takes to house veterans in the HUD-VASH program.

Alicia Puente Cackley
Director, Financial Markets and Community Investment

APPENDIX I. OBJECTIVES, SCOPE, AND METHODOLOGY

Our objectives were to examine (1) how the Department of Veterans Affairs (VA) and the Department of Housing and Urban Development (HUD) determine that veterans who participate in the HUD-VA Supportive Housing (HUD-VASH) program meet the statutory eligibility criteria, (2) what data VA and HUD collect and report on the HUD-VASH program and the steps that VA and HUD take to help ensure the reliability of these data, and (3) what is known about the performance of the HUD-VASH program.

To address all three objectives, we reviewed VA and HUD documents to determine the purpose of the HUD-VASH program and the agencies' roles and responsibilities related to HUD-VASH. In addition, we reviewed federal strategic plans that address veteran homelessness to obtain information on VA's and HUD's goals related to reducing veteran homelessness. We interviewed officials at the Veterans Health Administration within VA and in HUD's Office of Public and Indian Housing and Office of Community Planning and Development. We reviewed VA and HUD Office of Inspector General reports pertaining to HUD-VASH and our previous reports. We selected a purposive, non-representative sample of 10 locations in which to interview management and staff at VA medical centers (VAMC) and their partnering public housing agencies (PHA) (see figure 4). Results of these interviews cannot be projected to other VAMCs or PHAs. We selected the 10 locations (9 states and the District of Columbia) based on several criteria, including a significant presence of homeless veterans in and a large allocation of HUD-VASH vouchers to the state, identified best practices or challenges in administering the HUD-VASH program, and geographic diversity. To obtain information on the presence of homeless veterans by state, we reviewed the jointly developed veteran supplements to HUD's 2009 and 2010 Annual Homeless Assessment Reports to Congress. We used information from HUD on annual HUD-VASH voucher allocations by PHA and partnering VAMC for fiscal years 2008 through 2010.

To address our first objective, we reviewed eligibility requirements in the HUD-VASH statute to assess how VA and HUD are to determine that veterans who participate in HUD-VASH meet the statutory eligibility criteria. We also reviewed requirements specific to VA in the Veterans Health Administration's HUD-VASH handbook and a HUD-VASH resource guide developed by the National Center for Homelessness among Veterans.

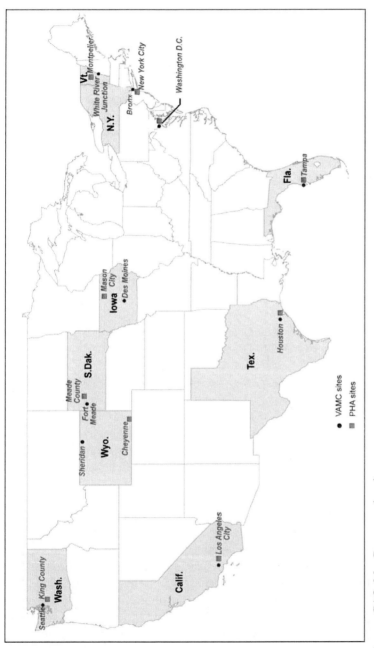

Source: GAO; Map Resources (map).

Figure 4. VA Medical Centers and Public Housing Agencies Contacted.

To obtain specific information on how VA screened veterans to determine if they were eligible for the program, we interviewed VAMC management and staff in the selected 10 locations. The centers are responsible for screening and evaluating veterans for acceptance into HUD-VASH, referring veterans to partnering PHAs, and coordinating veterans' case management under HUD-VASH. Similarly, to obtain more specific information on how PHAs (following HUD's procedures) screened veterans referred by partnering VAMCs, we interviewed management and staff at PHAs that partner with the 10 VAMCs to assess veterans and also manage various aspects of the housing process. In our interviews with VAMC and PHA staff, we asked about their general procedures for administering HUD-VASH, including how they made eligibility determinations based on VA's requirements and HUD's guidelines, respectively. We also discussed cooperation at the local level between partnering VAMCs and PHAs.

To address our second objective, we reviewed program manuals and guidance on data that VA and HUD collect on HUD-VASH, their data collection mechanisms, and reliability controls. We interviewed VA and HUD officials to determine what HUD-VASH information the agencies report and the systems they use for collecting and reporting the related data. We obtained and reviewed selected monthly Dashboard-based reports that VA provided to Congress during fiscal years 2011 and 2012 to identify the data elements typically reported for HUD-VASH; we reviewed VA program data through March 2012. While VA provides monthly voucher utilization reports to Congress, HUD reports to Congress on HUD-VASH only upon request. To identify the steps that VA takes to help ensure the reliability of its data, we interviewed knowledgeable VA officials about the purpose, structure, and quality controls used to capture or report HUD-VASH program data using VA's Dashboard and HOMES. We reviewed VA documentation, including the HOMES user manual, HUD-VASH data entry forms, and data validity checks. In interviews with VAMC staff at the 10 selected locations, we asked about data collection and reporting, and any related challenges. In addition, we observed a demonstration of VA's reporting mechanism for HUD-VASH on-site. Finally, we compared VA's data collection and reporting procedures to standards for internal control in the federal government. To identify the steps that HUD takes to help ensure the reliability of its data, we interviewed knowledgeable HUD officials about the purpose, structure, and relevant quality controls for HUD-VASH data, including information captured in HUD's Voucher Management System (VMS) and Public and Indian Housing Information Center (PIC). We also interviewed PHA staff at the 10 selected locations about data collection and reporting, and any related challenges. We reviewed relevant documentation, including the information systems' user guidance and HUD's documented analysis of comparisons between VMS, PIC, and VA data.

To address our third objective, we reviewed performance-related information reported by VA such as monthly Dashboard-based reports on HUD-VASH voucher utilization and a more descriptive report submitted to Congress in October 2011. In addition, we interviewed representatives of, and gathered documentation from, HUD and VA headquarters; the U.S. Interagency Council on Homelessness (Interagency Council); and veteran and homeless advocacy organizations, including the National Coalition for Homeless Veterans, the National Coalition for the Homeless, the National Alliance to End Homelessness, and Vietnam Veterans of America. In interviews with VA and HUD officials, we asked about performance measures the agencies were monitoring for HUD-VASH. In interviews with representatives of advocacy organizations, we discussed their perspectives on HUD-VASH administration and the program's performance. We also asked VAMC and PHA staff for their perspectives on HUD-VASH performance, potential ways to measure program success, and opportunities for improvement.

We conducted this performance audit from September 2011 through June 2012 in accordance with generally accepted government auditing standards. Those standards require that we plan and perform the audit to obtain sufficient, appropriate evidence to provide a reasonable basis for our findings and conclusions based on our audit objectives. We believe that the evidence obtained provides a reasonable basis for our findings and conclusions based on our audit objectives.

End Notes

[1] HUD and VA, *Veteran Homelessness: A Supplemental Report to the 2010 Annual Homeless Assessment Report to Congress* (Washington, D.C.: 2011).

[2] Communities annually submit point-in-time estimates to HUD. The counts attempt to enumerate both unsheltered persons (those in places not meant for human habitation such as the streets, abandoned buildings, or cars) and sheltered persons (those in emergency shelter or transitional housing on the night of the point-in-time count). Communities typically conduct their counts during a 24-hour period in the last week in January when a large share of the homeless population is expected to seek shelter rather than stay outside. The timing of the point-in-time count is intended to improve accuracy because counts of people in shelters are more precise than counts of people on the streets.

[3] A PHA is a local entity, typically created under state law, which receives funds from HUD to administer the voucher program. A family that is issued a housing voucher is responsible for finding a suitable housing unit of the family's choice which the owner agrees to rent under the program. A housing subsidy is paid to the landlord directly by the PHA on behalf of the family. The family pays the difference between the actual rent charged by the landlord and the amount subsidized by the program.

[4] More specifically, VA's data for "vouchers currently in use" represent the sum of totals from three categories: (1) vouchers reserved for veterans who are undergoing PHA validation, (2) vouchers issued to veterans who are actively seeking a lease, and (3) current veterans housed/under lease. The data represent voucher utilization at a point-in-time.

[5] According to HUD officials, HUD did not track HUD-VASH vouchers separately from general section 8 vouchers until the program was expanded in fiscal year 2008.

[6] These figures do not include HUD-VASH voucher obligations after the initial appropriation year of the vouchers. After the initial funding year, HUD-VASH vouchers are renewed via a funding formula used for regular section 8 vouchers and HUD does not report those obligations separately from other section 8 vouchers.

[7] According to VA officials, VA does not count its community-based outpatient clinics as separate entities for HUD-VASH administration. The clinics operate under a parent VA facility (such as a VAMC).

[8] PHAs participating in HUD-VASH from fiscal years 2008 through 2012 may not have been awarded vouchers for each fiscal year during that time frame.

[9] The McKinney-Vento Act, as amended per the HEARTH Act of 2009, defines a homeless individual to include "(1) an individual . . . who lacks a fixed, regular, and adequate nighttime residence; (2) an individual . . . with a primary nighttime residence that is a public or private place not designed for or ordinarily used as a regular sleeping accommodation for human beings . . . ; (3) an individual . . . living in a supervised publicly or privately operated shelter designed to provide temporary living accommodations . . .; (4) an individual who resided in a shelter or place not meant for human habitation and who is exiting an institution where he or she temporarily resided; (5) an individual . . . who (A) will imminently lose [his or her] housing. . . ; (B) has no subsequent residence identified; and (C) lacks the resources or support networks needed to obtain other permanent housing." 42 U.S.C. § 11302(a).

[10] VA health care is generally only available to a veteran enrolled in the VA health care system. The term veteran is defined in 38 U.S.C. § 101(2) as "a person who served in the active military, naval, or air service, and who was discharged or released there from under conditions other than dishonorable."

[11] The veteran must provide proof of qualifying income level. Typically, the veteran pays approximately 30 percent of the adjusted household income to the landlord and the PHA pays the remainder (the rental subsidy) up to a predetermined amount.

[12] More than 20 VISNs report to VA's national center. In 1995, the Veterans Health Administration established VISNs to oversee daily operations and decisions affecting hospitals, clinics, nursing homes, and veteran centers located within their regions. According to VA, VISNs remain the fundamental units for managing funding and ensuring accountability.

[13] According to VA, HOMES is a component of the Homeless Registry, the system which facilitates the actual HUD-VASH reporting functions. The Homeless Registry incorporates data collected through HOMES, legacy program evaluation data, VA benefits, administrative data, and data from the clinical records. According to one official, this registry is the foundation for the Homeless Services cube which allows numerous, multifaceted reporting, trending, aggregation, and dissection across time, location, programs and patient characteristics.

[14] Initially called the Comprehensive Service Programs, the Grant and Per Diem program was introduced as a pilot program in 1992 through the Homeless Veterans Comprehensive Services Act (Pub. L. No. 102-590). The law establishing the Grant and Per Diem program,

which was made permanent in the Homeless Veterans Comprehensive Services Act of 2001 (Pub. L. No. 107-95), authorizes VA to make grants to public entities or private nonprofit organizations to provide services and transitional housing to homeless veterans. Domiciliary care consists of rehabilitative services for physically and mentally ill or aged veterans who need assistance, but are not in need of the level of care offered by hospitals and nursing homes. Congress first provided funds for the Domiciliary Care program for homeless veterans in 1987 through a supplemental appropriations act (Pub. L. No. 100-71).

[15] PHAs that participate in HUD's Moving to Work demonstration program have the flexibility to design and test various approaches for providing and administering housing assistance that are intended to reduce costs or to provide incentives to families with children where the head of household is working or seeking employment opportunities. For example, Moving to Work PHAs can conduct less frequent recertifications for certain households living on fixed incomes. For more information on the Moving to Work demonstration program, see GAO, *Moving to Work Demonstration: Opportunities Exist to Improve Information and Monitoring* GAO-12-490 (Washington, D.C.: Apr. 19, 2012).

[16] See GAO, *Standards for Internal Control in the Federal Government*, GAO/AIMD-00-21 .3.1 (Washington, D.C.: November 1999).

[17] However, this review and validation is not incorporated in VA's monthly Dashboard reports due to time lags associated with HUD's reporting processes, according to agency officials.

[18] At the discretion of the VAMC and subject to program requirements, a HUD-VASH participant can move outside of the jurisdiction of the PHA that made the initial award as long as VA case management can be continued in the receiving PHA's jurisdiction.

[19] The Housing First model aims to provide rapid rehousing for homeless families and identifies the need for interventions and social services support after housing is secured.

[20] Under the American Recovery and Reinvestment Act (Pub. L. No. 111-5), $1.5 billion was appropriated for Homelessness Prevention and Rapid Re-Housing Program grants. The grants were distributed to communities and states to provide short- or medium-term rental assistance and relocation and stabilization services, including housing search, mediation or outreach to property owners, credit repair, security or utility deposits, utility payments, rental assistance for a final month at a location, moving cost assistance, case management, or other appropriate activities.

[21] The Supportive Services for Veteran Families program was established by the Veterans' Mental Health and Other Care Improvements Act of 2008. The program provides grants to private nonprofit organizations and consumer cooperatives that will coordinate or provide supportive services to very low-income veteran families residing in or transitioning to permanent housing.

[22] Under the voucher program (including HUD-VASH), PHAs are limited by law to using up to only twenty percent of their overall tenant-based voucher budget authority for project-based vouchers. 42 U.S.C. § 1437f(o)(13). HUD has the authority to grant a PHA's request to exceed the 20 percent limit for the purposes of project-basing HUD-VASH vouchers. In connection with the HUD-VASH annual appropriations since 2008, HUD has been authorized to waive (with a few exceptions) statutory and regulatory requirements applicable to the HUD-VASH program, "upon a finding by the Secretary [of HUD] that any such waivers. . . are necessary for the effective delivery and administration of such voucher assistance." *See, e.g.*, HUD's fiscal year 2012 appropriations, Pub. L. 112-55, 125 Stat. 552, 678-679 (2011).

In: Veteran Housing Assistance
Editor: Craig Del Monte

ISBN: 978-1-62417-369-1
© 2013 Nova Science Publishers, Inc.

Chapter 4

"WHO IS A VETERAN?"— BASIC ELIGIBILITY FOR VETERANS' BENEFITS[*]

Christine Scott

SUMMARY

A broad range of benefits are offered to veterans of the U.S. Armed Forces and to certain members of their families by the U.S. Department of Veterans Affairs (VA). Among these benefits are various types of financial assistance, including monthly cash payments to disabled veterans, health care, education, and housing benefits. Basic criteria must be met to be eligible to receive any of the benefits administered by the VA.

For a former servicemember to receive certain VA benefits, the person must have active U.S. military service for a minimum period of time and meet nature of discharge requirements. Some members of the National Guard and reserve components have difficulty meeting the active duty and length of service requirements. However, a member of the National Guard or reserve components who is activated for federal military service and serves the full period of activation is considered a veteran for purposes of VA benefits.

---

[*] This is an edited, reformatted and augmented version of the Congressional Research Service Publication, CRS Report for Congress R42324, dated January 23, 2012.

The GI Bill Improvement Act of 1977 (P.L. 95-202) recognized the service of one group of civilians, the Women's Air Forces Service Pilots, as active service for benefits administered by the VA, and it also established that the Secretary of Defense could determine that service for the Armed Forces by a group of civilians, or contractors, be considered active service for benefits administered by the VA.

This report examines the basic eligibility criteria for VA administered veterans' benefits, including the issue of eligibility of members of the National Guard and reserve components.

INTRODUCTION

A broad range of benefits are offered to veterans of the U.S. Armed Forces and to certain members of their families by the U.S. Department of Veterans Affairs (VA). Among these benefits are various types of financial assistance, including monthly cash payments to disabled veterans, health care, education, and housing benefits. Basic criteria must be met to be eligible to receive any of the benefits administered by the VA.

This report focuses upon the basic eligibility/entitlement requirements for former servicemembers for veterans' benefits administered by the VA. Certain VA benefits are available to current servicemembers, and the eligibility requirements for those benefits are not a component of this report.

The VA uses a two-step process to evaluate claims for benefits. First, the claimant must demonstrate that he or she is *eligible*. That is, the claimant must prove that he or she is a bona fide veteran and verify certain related matters. In this sense, the eligibility relates to the veteran's general qualification(s) for the benefit(s). Second, the veteran must prove *entitlement* to the particular benefit being sought.[1]

WHO IS A VETERAN?

To be eligible for most VA benefits, the claimant must be a veteran or, in some circumstances, the survivor or the dependent of a veteran. By statute, a "veteran" is defined as a "person who served in the active military, naval, or air service, and who was discharged or released therefrom under conditions other than dishonorable."[2]

In evaluating the evidence to determine whether the applicant is a "veteran" for the purposes of VA benefits, the VA relies upon military department service records. The VA is bound by information that the service documents contain.[3] Generally speaking, the VA findings will be in accord with the information contained in the applicant's military service records.[4]

Such records may include an original military service record; a copy issued by the military service with the certification that it is a true document; or a copy submitted by an accredited agent, attorney, or service representative with special training, who certifies that it is a copy of an original military service document or a copy of a copy of such a document.[5] In addition to meeting these criteria, the document must contain data regarding the length, time, and character of the service, and the VA must believe that the document is genuine and accurate.[6] If the claimant does not provide the requisite documentation or other evidence, or the submitted documentation does not meet the requirements, the VA must seek to verify the applicant's military service directly from the appropriate military service.[7]

Active Service

An applicant must have "active military, naval, or air service" to be considered a veteran for most VA benefits.[8] However, not all types of service are considered active military service for this purpose.[9]

In general, active service means full-time service, other than active duty for training, as a member of the Army, Navy, Air Force, Marine Corps, Coast Guard, or as a commissioned officer of the Public Health Service, the Environmental Science Services Administration or the National Oceanic and Atmospheric Administration, or its predecessor, the Coast and Geodectic Survey. Active service also includes a period of active duty for training during which the person was disabled or died from an injury or disease incurred or aggravated in the line of duty[10] and any period of inactive duty for training during which the person was disabled or died from an injury incurred or aggravated in the line of duty or from certain health conditions incurred during the training.[11] Additional circumstances of service, and whether they are deemed to be active military service, are set out in law.[12] For example, if on authorized travel to and from the performance of active duty training or inactive duty for training, a person is disabled or dies while proceeding directly to or returning from such duty, the duty will be considered to be active duty for training or inactive duty for training.[13] The determination of whether a claimant has met the "active service" requirement may not be a simple process. It is possible that the claimant and the VA may have to scrutinize the claimant's service record(s) to determine whether the claimant's service fits into one of the many categories of active service, or whether an exception has been made for his or her service, so that it is considered to be active service for the purposes of veterans' benefits. In addition, a claimant may have more than one period of service, which may further complicate the determination.

Length of Service

Prior to September 8, 1980, there was no minimum length of service necessary to be considered a veteran for most VA benefits. However, for an individual who enlisted after September 8, 1980, there are now certain minimum length of service requirements. The general requirement is either 24 months of continuous active duty or the "full period" for which the servicemember was called or ordered to active duty.[14]

Several exceptions exist to this general rule. For example, service-connected disability compensation benefits are exempt from the minimum active duty requirements. Thus, a veteran with a disease or injury incurred during active service should almost always be able to receive service-connected compensation for his or her condition or disability.[15] Other exceptions to the minimum service requirements include claims for VA life insurance benefits,[16] hardship discharges,[17] and persons retired or separated from service because of a service-related disability.[18]

If the former servicemember does not fall within the 24 months of active duty or the "full period" of active duty, or within one of the statutory exceptions, then the veteran has not completed a minimum period of active duty and is "not eligible for any benefit under Title 38, United States Code or under any law administered by the Department of Veterans Affairs based on that period of active service."[19]

Discharge Criteria

The statutory definition of "veteran" requires that the individual be discharged or released from military service "under conditions other than dishonorable."[20] There are currently five types of discharges issued by the military services: (1) honorable discharge (HD), (2) discharge under honorable conditions (UHC) or general discharge (GD), (3) discharge under other than honorable conditions (UOTHC) or undesirable discharge (UD), (4) bad conduct discharge (BCD), and (5) dishonorable discharge (DD).[21]

The language of the statute does not precisely match the current categories of the discharges, and the VA often determines on a case-by-case basis whether the claimant's discharge satisfies any of the criteria and which category of discharge applies. In most cases, the VA considers honorable discharges and discharges under honorable conditions to fall within the "conditions other than dishonorable" category, and will usually qualify the claimant as a veteran under the first step of the eligibility test.[22] Usually, honorable and general discharges qualify a veteran for most benefits.[23]

A bad conduct discharge from a special court-martial and other discharges made under other than honorable conditions may or may not disqualify the claimant from being considered a veteran for purposes of benefits eligibility.[24] In the case of such a discharge, the VA will make a special "character of service determination," based on the particular facts in the claimant's case. On this basis, the VA will determine whether the veteran was separated from service under "dishonorable conditions" or under "other than dishonorable conditions." The VA will review the entire period of the claimant's enlistment(s) to assess the quality of the service and to determine whether it is sufficient to deserve the award of veterans' benefits.[25] If a claimant has served more than one period of enlistment, he or she may have two or more different discharge categories.

Dishonorable and bad conduct discharges issued by general courts-martial may bar VA benefits. Veterans in prison and parolees may be eligible for certain VA benefits and must contact the VA to determine eligibility. VA benefits will not be provided to any veteran or dependent wanted for an outstanding felony warrant.

Certain exceptions permit the award of VA benefits, even if the character of the discharge would ordinarily bar VA benefits. For example, if it is determined that the claimant was insane at the time of the offense leading up to the discharge, the claimant may be granted VA benefits. There does not need to be a direct connection between the insanity and the misconduct.[26]

Whether the Military Service Was during a Time of War[27]

All military service is classified as either wartime or peacetime service. Whether a veteran has served during a time of war may impact his or her potential VA benefits. For example, the Improved Pension benefit for low-income veterans who are either elderly or non-service-connected disabled veterans, is only for veterans with wartime service.[28]

Congress has set out the periods of "wartime" for the purposes of veterans' benefits.[29] To be considered to have "served during wartime" by the VA, a veteran does not have to have served in an actual combat zone, but during the specified periods of war set out below. Those time periods not designated by Congress as "wartime" are considered to be "peacetime." If a veteran served his or her duty partly during wartime and partly during peacetime, the veteran would meet the "wartime" criteria if he or she served 90 consecutive days, at least one day of which occurred during a period designated as wartime.

Following is a list of those periods of "wartime" designated by Congress:

- *Indian Wars*—January 1, 1817, through December 31, 1898[30]
- *Spanish-American War*—April 21, 1898, through July 4, 1902[31]
- *Mexican Border Period*—May 19, 1916, though April 5, 1917[32]
- *World War I*—April 6, 1917, through November 11, 1918; extended to April 1, 1920; by regulation extended to July 1, 1921, under certain specific conditions[33]
- *World War II*—December 7, 1941, through December 31, 1946; extended to July 25, 1947[34]
- *Korean Conflict*—June 27, 1950, through January 31, 1955[35]
- *Vietnam Era*—August 5, 1964, through May 7, 1975[36]
- *Persian Gulf War*—August 2, 1990, through a date to be prescribed by Presidential proclamation or law[37]

NATIONAL GUARD AND RESERVE

Two particular elements of the criteria to be a veteran—"active duty" and "length of service"— are often difficult for members of the National Guard and the reserve components to meet. As a result, these servicemembers, having not met the statutory threshold criteria for "veteran," are often not eligible for VA benefits.

In many cases, members of the Guard and the reserves may not have fulfilled the "active duty" requirement. Members of the Guard and reserves who have never been activated for federal active duty military service, and consequently have not served on regular federal active duty, do not meet the active duty requirement for the definition of a veteran for VA benefits.

For other National Guard and reserve members, the two requirements may be met at the same time. An example of this situation would be a Guard or reserve member who was activated for federal military service and served in the Persian Gulf for 12 months. At the end of the activation period, the servicemember would be considered to have served on active duty for that period of time. Serving for the full period of activation also meets the minimum length of service requirement to be a veteran. Otherwise, Guard and reserve duty may not be considered "active duty" for benefits unless the servicemember performing this duty was disabled or died from a disease or injury incurred or aggravated in the line of duty.[38]

Although many National Guard and reserve members may not appear to be eligible "veterans" for the purposes of VA benefits, certain exceptions and special circumstances may exist, which add to the complexity of the eligibility determination. For example, under certain conditions Guard and reserve members may be eligible for education benefits (through the Reserve Educational Program or the Post-9/11 GI Bill) and home loans from the VA (with six years of service in the Selected Reserves or National Guard). As each servicemember's military service may be different, and therefore may fit within certain case categories or exceptions, eligibility is usually determined by the VA on a case-by-case basis after reviewing the individual servicemember's military service records.

CIVILIAN GROUPS

The GI Bill Improvement Act of 1977 (P.L. 95-202) recognized the service of one group of civilians, the Women's Air Forces Service Pilots, as active service for benefits administered by the U.S. Department of Veterans Affairs. In addition, P.L. 95-202 provided that the Secretary of Defense could determine that service for the Armed Forces by a group of civilians, or contractors, be considered active service for benefits administered by the VA.

Based on the provisions of P.L. 95-202,[39] the Secretary of Defense established that the Secretary of the Air Force would develop and maintain the process to determine if the wartime employment of certain groups of individuals is considered "active duty" military service for the purpose of receiving certain veterans benefits. If these groups of individuals are considered to be "active duty" by the Secretary, they are eligible to receive certain benefits, including health care.[40]

Regulations implementing P.L. 95-202 specify which groups the Secretary has determined were employed in "active duty" service.[41] The regulations also established the Department of Defense Civilian/Military Service Review Board and Advisory Panel to review each application for "active duty" status.[42] Following its review, the board issues a written recommendation to the Secretary as to whether the applicant group should be considered "active duty" for the purposes of the act. The Secretary makes the final decision, based upon the recommendation of the board. Pursuant to this procedure, various groups of persons have been accorded "active duty" status. Among the successful applicants were Women's Air Forces Service Pilots (WASPs), Signal Corps Female Telephone Operators Unit (World War I), Engineer Field Clerks (World War I), Male Civilian Ferry Pilots (World War II), and other groups of employees with war-related occupations.[43] At this time, all of the successful applicants have been civilian groups associated with World War I and World War II.

The regulations concerning the designation of "active duty" status have undergone revision over the years. Changes and clarification to the regulations implemented in 1989 "stem from a Federal Court determination [*Schumacher v. Aldridge*][44] that the Department of Defense had failed to clarify factors and criteria in their implementing directive concerning P.L. 95-202."[45] The 1989 regulations remain in effect.

End Notes

[1] For example, to be entitled to receive disability compensation, a veteran must provide sufficient evidence of certain elements (e.g., current diagnosis, medical evidence of an in-service occurrence, and link between the in-service occurrence and the current disability).

[2] 38 U.S.C. § 101(2); 38 C.F.R. § 3.1(d).

[3] Venturella v. Gober, 10 Vet. App. 340, 341-342 (1977); Duro v. Derwinski, 2 Vet. App. 530, 532 (1992).

[4] 38 C.F.R. § 3.203.

[5] 38 C.F.R. § 3.203(a)(1). See CRS Report RS21282, *Military Service Records and Unit Histories: A Guide to Locating Sources*, by Julissa Gomez-Granger and Anne Leland.

[6] 38 C.F.R. § 3.203(a)(2), (3).

[7] Duro, 2 Vet. App. at 532.

[8] 38 U.S.C. § 101(2); 38 C.F.R. § 3.12(a).

[9] For example, National Guard and Reserve duty may not be considered active service unless an individual performing this duty was disabled or died from a disease or injury incurred or aggravated in the line of duty. (38 U.S.C. § 101(24); 38 C.F.R. § 3.6(a)).

[10] Active duty for training is a tour of active duty that is used for training members of reserve and other components to fill the Armed Forces during time of war or national emergency. Active duty for training has been determined to mean (1) full-time duty for training performed by Reservists (38 U.S.C. § 101(22)(A); 38 C.F.R. § 3.6(c)(1)); (2) full-time duty for training purposes as a commissioned officer in the Reserved Corps of the Public Health Service (38 U.S.C. § 101(22)(B); 38 C.F.R. § 3.6(c)(2)); (3) full-time training duty by members of the Air or Army National Guard of any state (38 U.S.C. § 101(22)(C); 38 C.F.R. § 3.6(c)(3)); (4) duty by members of the Senior ROTC program on field training or a practice cruise (38 U.S.C. § 101 (22)(D); 38 C.F.R. § 3.6(c)(4)); and (5) authorized travel to and from duty for training (38 U.S.C. § 101(22)(E); 38 C.F.R. § 3.6(c)(6)).

[11] 38 U.S.C. § 101(24). Inactive duty for training has been defined to mean (1) duty, other than full-time duty, for Reservists (38 U.S.C. § 101(23)(A); 38 C.F.R. § 3.6(d)(1)); (2) other duties authorized for Reservists performed on a voluntary basis (38 U.S.C. § 101(23)(B); 38 C.F.R. § 3.6(d)(2)); (3) training (other than active duty for training) by a member of, or applicant for membership in, Senior ROTC (38 U.S.C. § 101(23)(C); 38 C.F.R. § 3.6(d)(3)); and (4) for the members of the Air or Army National Guard of any state, such training means duty other than full-time duty (38 U.S.C. § 101(23); 38 C.F.R. § 3.6(d)(4)).

[12] 38 U.S.C. §§ 101, 106.

[13] 38 U.S.C. § 106(d); 38 C.F.R. § 3.6(e).

[14] 38 U.S.C. § 5303A(b); 38 C.F.R. § 3.12a(a)(1).

[15] 38 U.S.C. § 5303A(b)(3)(C); 38 C.F.R. § 3.12a(d)(4).

[16] 38 U.S.C. § 5303A(b)(3)(E); 38 C.F.R. § 3.12a(d)(5).

[17] 38 U.S.C. § 5303A(b)(3)(A); 38 C.F.R. § 3.12a(d)(1).

[18] 38 U.S.C. § 5303A(b)(3)(B); 38 C.F.R. § 3.12a(d)(2).

[19] 38 U.S.C. § 5303A(b)(1); 38 C.F.R. § 3.12a(b).

[20] 38 U.S.C. § 101(2); 38 C.F.R. § 3.12(a).

[21] Barton F. Stichman et al., *Veterans Benefits Manual*, at § 2.2.1 (Cited to afterward as "Veterans Benefits Manual").

[22] Ibid.

[23] Ibid.

[24] Ibid.

[25] Ibid.

[26] 38 U.S.C. § 5303(b).

[27] See CRS Report RS21405, *U.S. Periods of War and Dates of Current Conflicts*, by Barbara Salazar Torreon.

[28] 38 U.S.C. § 1521(j).

[29] 38 U.S.C. § 101 (6)-(11); 38 C.F.R. § 3.2.

[30] See 38 C.F.R. § 3.2(a).

[31] 38 U.S.C. § 101(6); 38 C.F.R. § 3.2(b).

[32] 38 U.S.C. § 101(30); 38 C.F.R. § 3.2(h).

[33] 38 U.S.C. § 101(7); 38 C.F.R. § 3.2(c).

[34] 38 U.S.C. § 101(8); 38 C.F.R. § 3.2(d).

[35] 38 U.S.C. § 101(9); 38 C.F.R. § 3.2(e).

[36] 38 U.S.C. § 101(29); 38 C.F.R. § 3.2(f). Military personnel who served in the Republic of Vietnam between February 28, 1961, and May 7, 1975, are also considered to have served during the Vietnam Era.

[37] 38 U.S.C. §§ 101(33), 1501(4); 38 C.F.R. §§ 3.2(I), 3.3(a)(3), 3.17, 3.54(a)(3)(viii). At the present time, no termination date has been established.

[38] 38 U.S.C. § 101(21)(A); 38 C.F.R. § 3.6(a). Inactive duty would include duty other than full-time duty, such as weekend assignments or part-time details.

[39] 38 U.S.C. § 106 note.
[40] See 38 C.F.R. § 3.7.
[41] 32 C.F.R. § 47. See 38 C.F.R. § 3.7 for those groups that have been so designated.
[42] The applications are usually submitted by representatives of the employment group.
[43] 38 C.F.R. § 3.7.
[44] 665 F.Supp. 41 (D.D.C. 1987).
[45] 54 *Fed.* Reg. 39,991 (September 29, 1989).

INDEX